Stress-Free Travel

Insider Tips for Efficient Planning

PUBLISHED BY: Patrick Karban

Translated from German by myself as part of my translation work.

Table of Contents:

Patrick Karban

Introduction

For many people, traveling is one of the best ways to discover new cultures, escape from everyday life and gain valuable experiences. Millions of people worldwide travel yearly - for vacation, business or adventure. According to statistics, there are over 70 million vacation trips annually in Germany alone, and the trend is rising. But as exciting as traveling is, it often comes with challenges that can make the experience stressful: unexpected delays, health problems, language barriers and much more.

This is precisely where this book comes in. It is designed to help travelers make their trips efficient, stress-free and healthy, from planning to return. Whether you're planning a city break, a business trip or an adventure trip lasting several weeks - with the right strategies and thoughtful preparation, your trip will be smoother and more enjoyable. With practical tips and structured approaches, this book is a valuable resource for seasoned explorers and adventurers embarking on their first trip.

Planning a trip that meets your expectations while staying within your comfort zone is often a challenge when you want to immerse yourself in the endless world of travel. This book helps travelers of all experience levels plan their trip, from destination selection to time management, and is aimed at both seasoned explorers and first-time adventurers.

Travel is one of the most enriching experiences our lives have to offer. However, planning a trip can often be stressful and frustrating. Time is a limited resource for busy professionals, and it may initially seem impossible to make time for careful travel planning. On the other hand, despite their desire to explore, avid travelers can benefit significantly from practical strategies to make their trips smoother and more enjoyable. This book aims to bridge the gap between dreams and reality and give valuable tips to make your travel dreams come true through well-organized adventures.

Imagine standing on a pristine beach at sunset and feeling the warmth of the sand on your feet or wandering through old, winding streets and discovering hidden highlights you won't find in any travel guide. This is precisely what we are looking for when we travel. But behind each of these experiences is a well-thought-out travel plan that considers every detail, from the choice of destination to the correct time frame for your stay. This book shows you how to experience such moments without any problems. This way, you can return home with experiences that will last a lifetime and avoid frustration and regrets.

We start our journey with the question of choosing the perfect destination. Whether you crave tranquil landscapes, bustling cities or cultural spots, finding a place that suits your interests and budget is essential. You'll get tips on researching destinations, evaluating travel advice and understanding local customs and climate to make an informed decision that suits your travel style.

Next, we'll look at the art of packing efficiently. As the saying goes, "less is more," which applies to traveling. By mastering the art of packing, you can avoid unnecessary stress and instead focus on your upcoming adventure. Learn how to assemble suitable outfits, gather essential items, and use packing aids that save space and store your belongings neatly.

The choice of accommodation is another crucial aspect that can determine the success or failure of your trip. Whether you're considering luxury hotels, cozy bed and breakfasts or unique accommodations like treehouses and boutique hostels, this book offers valuable insight into choosing the best lodging options to suit your needs and preferences. You'll get tips on reading reviews critically, booking at the right time, and using loyalty programs to enhance your stay without going over budget.

A well-planned itinerary ensures a good balance between the most important sights and relaxing moments. You will receive recommendations on optimizing your schedule, avoiding tourist traps and incorporating spontaneous activities that will make your trip extra special. Effective time management ensures you get the most out of your travels while leaving room for surprising experiences.

Effective budget planning is essential for every traveler, regardless of financial constraints. This book is about managing your money wisely, keeping an eye on your spending and finding ways to save money - with practical tips and real-life examples. Travel doesn't have to be expensive to offer great experiences. With the right approach, you can use your budget more effectively than you imagined.

In each chapter, you'll find sections dedicated to overcoming common travel obstacles. From dealing with delays and cancellations to handling health and safety issues, these insights will prepare you to tackle unexpected challenges with confidence and ease. The goal is to provide you with the foresight and tools to ensure that unforeseen events are accounted for on your trip.

By delving into the intricacies of travel planning described in the following pages, you can gain valuable knowledge to optimize your travel preparations and overcome potential challenges. Whether you want to maximize your travel budget, improve your itinerary or take the stress out of travel planning, this book is a valuable companion for your explorations.

Throughout the book, you'll find anecdotal experiences from other travelers who have successfully implemented and benefited from these strategies. Their stories inspire and prove that thoughtful preparation enhances the quality of travel experiences. Whether it's a business trip extended into a personal vacation or a long-awaited vacation that exceeds expectations, this book will show you the impact that effective travel planning can have.

This book is not just a guide but a guidebook with practical tips tailored to the needs of today's travelers. You'll also get access to checklists and templates to simplify your planning process. With these tools, you can turn what used to feel like a lot of work into an exciting start to your trip.

Have a good trip!

Practical Realization

This book is essentially dedicated to the theoretical aspects of successful travel planning. But sometimes, theoretical advice can seem abstract and difficult to grasp. I decided to create a fictional character: Sarah, to close this gap and make the tips and strategies more understandable and practical. She will guide you through the book and describe after each chapter how the tips and procedures mentioned can be applied to your next trip.

Sarah serves as a companion who puts the theoretical knowledge into practice so that you, the reader, can see how the individual pieces of advice are applied in reality. Of course, it may not be able to represent every single reader exactly, as everyone has different backgrounds and travel destinations. But Sarah is representative of many of us who plan our trips carefully to get the most out of every experience. Her social status or merits play a subordinate role - instead, Sarah makes the theoretical concepts tangible and focuses on the actual advice.

Through their experiences, you can understand how you can apply the chapters' tips to your travels. Sarah shows no perfect formula for traveling but that flexible and thoughtful planning is the key to a successful travel experience.

Here is the profile of Sarah:

Name: Sarah Thompson

Age: 29

Gender: Female

Relationship status: Single

Family situation: No children

Previous travel experience: Moderate (traveled to more than 10 countries)

Average income: €60,000 / year

Professional background: Corporate lawyer

Interests: History, cultural events, wellness stays

Other important facts: Prefers structured itineraries, likes to travel alone or with close friends

Brief description: Sarah is a dedicated corporate lawyer passionate about history and culture. She loves to immerse herself in new environments and learn more about local traditions. Although her job is demanding, she makes time for wellness breaks and cultural trips. Sarah values well-organized travel planning and often looks for package tours that suit her interests and allow her to relax and recharge her batteries without the stress of detailed planning. Nevertheless, she appreciates the flexibility of controlling her travel planning from start to finish.

Chapter 1: Choose Your Perfect Destination

Choosing the perfect destination involves much more than just wanting to travel to a specific place, as there are several important factors to consider. Every traveler has preferences and needs, from personal interests to practical aspects such as safety and budget. Choosing the ideal destination starts with understanding these different needs and matching them with the characteristics of the other destinations.

In this chapter, we'll look at choosing a destination that suits your interests: outdoor adventures, cultural experiences or relaxing getaways. We will also discuss how different environments affect your experience and how evaluating these circumstances can improve your overall satisfaction. By the end of this chapter, you will have a clear overview of how to find a destination that will inspire you and meet your needs efficiently and safely.

Assessing Personal Interests and Preferences

Busy professionals and travel enthusiasts can enhance their travel experiences by combining their desired destinations with their hobbies and passions.

First, think about which goals match your hobbies. If you like hiking, national parks offer an ideal environment for exploration and adventure. National parks such as Yellowstone or Yosemite in the United States offer breathtaking landscapes and numerous hiking trails where hiking enthusiasts get their money's worth. For water sports enthusiasts, coastal regions or islands such as the Maldives or Hawaii are ideal for surfing, snorkeling and diving. Choosing a destination that suits your hobbies will ensure you stay active and interested in your surroundings during your trip.

In addition, researching cultural activities and historical sites can further enhance your travel experience. Many travelers find that immersing themselves in the local culture gives them a deeper understanding and appreciation of the destination. Cities steeped in history, like Rome, have veritable treasure troves of museums, ancient ruins, and architectural marvels. The Vatican Museums, for example, offer a journey through centuries of art and history. Taking part in local cultural activities, such as traditional cooking classes or dance lessons, further enriches the experience as you get to know the traditions and lifestyle of the region first-hand. This approach makes your journey more meaningful, contributes to personal development, and broadens your horizons by fostering a greater sense of global diversity and empathy.

The surroundings are another critical factor when choosing a destination. Some travelers feel most comfortable in specific environments. Therefore, considering whether you prefer coastal areas or mountain regions can significantly impact your stay. Seaside resorts such as Santorini offer beautiful beaches, a mild climate and plenty of opportunities for water-based activities. In contrast, mountain regions such as the Swiss Alps offer picturesque landscapes, skiing opportunities and quiet hiking trails. When you find out which landscapes appeal to you the most, planning your trip becomes an individual experience that combines relaxation and adventure.

One practical aspect to consider is how the cost of your interests will affect your travel budget. Different activities are associated with other costs, which you must consider when planning your trip. For example, diving trips to places like the Great Barrier Reef can be expensive due to equipment rental fees, professional guides and the certificates that are sometimes required. On the other hand, hiking is a relatively budget-friendly activity that requires only minimal expenditure apart from the right equipment. In addition, entrance fees are often charged for cultural activities such as museum visits, which are usually reasonable but can quickly add up if you visit several places. If you thoroughly assess the costs of your chosen activities, you can better manage your travel budget and avoid financial difficulties.

Knowing your interests and preferences is essential to creating unforgettable travel experiences. The first step is to do some soul-searching and discover what excites you. Ask yourself questions like: Do I enjoy outdoor adventures? Am I fascinated by history and culture? Would I instead relax on the beach or explore bustling cities? These considerations form the basis for selecting destinations that meet your requirements. A good approach is to list your three most essential interests and look for destinations that match these interests. This way, you can narrow the selection and tailor your trip to your interests.

The next step is to align the activities with your interests. If you like taking photos, you should prefer destinations with breathtaking landscapes or lively street life. Places like Iceland, with its spectacular waterfalls and the Northern Lights, are a true paradise for photographers. The choice could also fall on countries known for their culinary delights, such as Italy or Japan. Participating in local food tours, visiting markets and cooking classes can make a food-focused trip particularly rewarding. If you design your itinerary to include activities that match your interests, you can be sure that every moment of your journey will be enjoyable and satisfying.

Although environmental aspects are not a direct factor in the choice of destination, they play an essential role in improving the travel experience. The environment you immerse yourself in dramatically impacts your mood and happiness on the trip. Whether it's the calming waves of a coastal city or the fresh air of the mountains, choosing a location that suits your environmental preferences can make your trip more enjoyable and memorable.

Finally, it would be best to consider your budget limits when planning your activities. Some destinations offer activities that are perfect but may not fit into your budget. A realistic assessment of what you can afford will ensure that your trip remains stress-free and financially manageable. Drawing up a travel budget with cost estimates for accommodation, meals, transportation and activities helps to avoid overspending. This makes for a more relaxed and enjoyable travel experience. In a later chapter, we will go into more detail about determining your travel budget.

If you have made a list of the aspects your destination must fulfill in any case, creating a shortlist of 5 destination countries can be helpful if you find it challenging to decide. From here you can compare more precisely which destination most closely overlaps with your preferences.

Assessment of Travel Restrictions and Safety

Several factors are essential in choosing a safe destination, all contributing to a safe and enjoyable trip. Ensuring safety when traveling is the be-all and end-all. It starts with thorough research and awareness of the potential risks associated with any destination.

First, you should read the travel advice and current news about possible dangers such as crime or terrorism in the country you are traveling to. For example, the U.S. State Department issues travel advisories that range from Level 1 (take standard precautions) to Level 4 (do not travel) and provide a clear overview of the security situation in various countries (U.S. State Department Travel Advisories, n.d.). In addition, the Foreign Office in Germany also provides a wide range of information online on many aspects of security for every destination. Travelers may feel more comfortable in Andorra, for example, rated Level 1 in the US, due to its stable and safe environment. In countries such as Angola, which are listed under level 2, increased caution is required as violent crime is more frequent there, and medical care is inadequate, especially outside the major cities.

In addition to the travel advice, you must learn about the medical requirements and healthcare quality at your destination. You should also check whether your health insurance covers you in the country in question or whether you should take out additional travel insurance. Certain vaccinations may be required or recommended depending on the diseases prevalent locally. For example, Cholera, typhoid and schistosomiasis are often a problem in regions with poor sanitary facilities and limited access to clean water. Vaccinations against these diseases can protect travelers from severe illness and maintain their health throughout their trip (Government of Canada, 2012).

It is also essential to know the political stability of a destination. Political unrest can significantly affect the safety and enjoyment of a trip. Government or social upheaval changes can lead to unpredictable situations that directly affect travelers. In Nigeria, for example, there is considerable unrest in various regions due to terrorism, crime and conflict between different population groups, causing travelers to avoid non-essential travel to most parts of the country (Government of Canada, 2012). If you know of such conditions through government warnings, you can make informed decisions about continuing or reconsidering your travel plans.

An often overlooked aspect of travel safety is to familiarize yourself with cultural norms to avoid accidental missteps leading to conflict or misunderstandings. Cultural sensitivity is the key to respectful interaction and can significantly improve your travel experience. For example, certain destinations have specific dress codes or behavioral expectations that travelers should adhere to. Understanding these norms allows you to blend seamlessly into the local culture without offending it or attracting unwanted attention. Simple measures, such as dressing modestly in conservative cultures or not showing affection in public, can ensure personal safety and encourage positive interactions with locals.

If you want to plan which countries you should visit or avoid in the long term, listing all the countries in the world is helpful. From here, you can refer to the previously mentioned sources, such as travel advice and safety ratings, and categorize the countries using a traffic light system to give you a good overview. Countries that fall into the red category are those in which there are often severe security problems such as armed conflicts, terrorism or high crime rates. It is best to avoid such countries, as the risks for tourists are disproportionately high. Countries such as Syria and Afghanistan are typical examples where political instability and the risk of violence or attacks would make travel an unpredictable adventure.

In contrast, green countries are particularly safe destinations. These countries offer travelers a high level of security, stable political systems and low crime rates. Japan and Canada are excellent examples of this. Both countries offer a rich culture, breathtaking landscapes and reliable infrastructure, so as a traveler there, you generally don't have to worry too much about your safety. These countries are also ideal for solo travelers or families.

Countries that are classified as yellow require you to exercise increased caution. This does not mean you should not travel there, but it is advisable to be well prepared and avoid certain regions or activities. A typical example of this is Mexico. While tourist areas such as Cancun or Playa del Carmen are mainly safe, there are other parts of the country, especially in the north, which are notable for their high crime rates, drug wars and kidnappings. Egypt also belongs in this category. While the pyramids of Giza and the temples of Luxor are popular and relatively safe destinations, there can be unrest in times of political tension, which you should keep an eye on.

The countries in orange are currently considered riskier but are still worth considering due to their cultural or scenic attractions. These countries often offer unforgettable experiences you don't want to miss, even if avoiding certain regions or times is advisable. A good example is the Bahamas. Although they are known for their iconic beaches and crystal clear waters, there are reports of increasing crime in certain parts of the country. Nevertheless, it remains a sought-after destination that attracts many travelers. The situation is similar in Haiti, where the fascinating voodoo culture and rich historical treasures contrast with an unstable political situation and high crime rate.

Countries such as India, Nepal and Peru also fall into this category. India offers impressive cultural diversity and historical sites such as the Taj Mahal. Still, it requires a certain amount of preparation, as some regions can have high crime and hygiene problems. On the other hand, Nepal attracts visitors with its unique Himalayan landscape and trekking opportunities. Still, the unstable infrastructure and earthquake risk make it a country where you must be careful. Peru attracts many travelers with Machu Picchu and the history of the Incas, but in some regions, there are safety issues that you should check carefully in advance.

Kenya and Jamaica are also among the countries impressed with their cultural and scenic highlights, but they require caution. You can experience unforgettable safaris in Kenya, but you should monitor the security situation in certain parts of the country. Jamaica offers Caribbean flair and a lively music scene, but there are problems with drug-related crime and violence in some cities.

These orange-rated countries are often the ones you keep on your travel list, even if you might want to be a little more flexible with the timing of your trip. If security improves, you can adjust your plans and visit these destinations without taking unnecessary risks.

Using Technology and Apps to Explore and Select Destinations

One of the most important aspects of modern travel planning is using digital tools to make the process less stressful and more efficient for working professionals and travel enthusiasts. With the wealth of online resources available, choosing the perfect destination can be exciting and straightforward.

On the one hand, social media platforms such as Instagram and Pinterest have become treasure troves of travel inspiration. Users can discover stunning images and posts from travelers worldwide that visually motivate them to explore new and unique places. Influencers and travel bloggers often share personal experiences, tips and hidden gems in their posts, making these platforms both a source of inspiration and a practical starting point for your travel research (5 Ways to Use Social Media for Travel Planning, n.d.).

Travel blogs and vlogs on YouTube are another excellent resource for potential travelers. These platforms offer detailed reviews, itineraries and illustrative tours to help you better understand potential destinations. Bloggers and vloggers often give honest insights into what you can expect, which can help you set realistic expectations and avoid common pitfalls. Reading about other people's first-hand experiences or watching a video about a destination will give you a better idea of whether it matches your preferences and interests.

Regarding digital tools, travel planning apps such as Google Trips and TripAdvisor are indispensable for organizing trips. These apps help users to create travel plans, manage reservations and even offer recommendations for activities, restaurants and accommodation. A significant advantage of these apps is the ability to harmonize different elements of your trip and ensure that all the necessary information is conveniently available in one place. This coordination benefits busy professionals who must manage their time efficiently and minimize planning stress.

Review and booking platforms such as Airbnb and Expedia are essential for making informed decisions. They provide user-generated reviews and ratings that help travelers assess the quality and reliability of accommodations, restaurants and attractions. If many verified users provide positive feedback about a particular service or location, this increases credibility and gives potential guests peace of mind. This transparency allows travelers to make informed decisions based on real experiences and not just promotional materials (Step-by-Step Guide to Developing Your Own Travel Planner App, n.d.).

To use these digital tools effectively, you must know how and how best to deploy them. For example, if you're looking for inspiration on social media, it's helpful to follow specific hashtags related to your interests, such as #beachvacation or #mountainlandscape. This strategy helps to reduce the vast range of relevant entries. If you save or bookmark exciting posts, you will have a collection of ideas for planning. We will discuss these aspects and tools for travel planning in more detail in later chapters.

When searching for information from travel blogs and vlogs, you must choose sources that suit your travel style and preferences. For example, if you are interested in adventure travel, you can follow bloggers specializing in hiking, camping or extreme sports to find more relevant offers. The exchange with these blogs and vlogs via comments or interactions on social media can also lead to personal advice and recommendations from experienced travelers.

Travel planning apps are most effective when used to their full potential. Entering all the necessary information, such as flight details, hotel reservations, and activity bookings, ensures that your itinerary is comprehensive and easy to follow. Many apps also offer features such as offline access to maps and travel guides, which can be invaluable in areas with limited internet connectivity.

Review and booking platforms not only help you choose the right accommodation but also find suitable transportation options and local attractions. Comparing reviews on different platforms can provide a balanced overview and help identify consistent patterns, whether positive or negative. It is also beneficial to look for recent reviews, as they reflect the current status of services and offers.

Integrating technology into your travel planning goes beyond choosing a destination. As the journey progresses, these digital aids offer support and flexibility. Real-time updates from travel apps can inform you of flight schedule changes or unexpected weather conditions so you can quickly adjust your plans. Social media can be a way to share experiences and get advice from other travelers, which improves the overall travel experience.

Combining these tools can create a seamless planning process for those who prefer a more structured approach. Start on social media for inspiration, and then browse travel blogs and vlogs for more information. Use travel planning apps to organize and set your itinerary, and rely on review and booking platforms to ensure the experiences of others support your decisions.

Exploring Up-and-Coming and LGBTQ-Friendly Destinations

Discovering unique and inclusive destinations can make your trip unforgettable. Emerging destinations offer a blend of novelty and welcoming environments that meet the diverse needs of travelers who want to explore off the beaten path while valuing inclusion.

Ljubljana and Medellín are excellent examples of such up-and-coming destinations. Ljubljana, the capital of Slovenia, is often described as an insider tip in Europe. This small but charming town is impressive with its picturesque streets, medieval castle, and lively cultural scene. The focus on sustainability and green spaces makes it attractive for environmentally conscious travelers. The notorious Medellín in Colombia has also developed remarkably over the years. Once infamous for drugs, the city is celebrated for its innovation, thriving arts scene and warm hospitality. Visiting these up-and-coming hotspots rewards you with unique experiences and the opportunity to contribute to tourism development positively.

For LGBTQ+ travelers, cities known for their inclusivity offer safety and a sense of belonging. Amsterdam and San Francisco are way ahead of their time in this respect. With its progressive politics and rich history of LGBTQ+ rights, Amsterdam offers a variety of queer-friendly spaces, from historic bars to modern cultural venues. San Francisco's Castro District also stands for the city's pioneering role in LGBTQ+ rights and acceptance and offers numerous stores and events specifically aimed at the community. These cities stand for diversity, making them safe and enjoyable for all travelers.

Safety is the most important when choosing a destination, especially for LGBTQ+ travelers. Resources like Equaldex and consulate information can help you navigate the local laws and social climate. Equaldex provides comprehensive data on LGBTQ+ rights worldwide, enabling you to assess how welcoming a country is. The consulates provide up-to-date safety advice and legal information to ensure your trip goes smoothly. If you learn about these aspects before booking your trip, you can avoid unpleasant surprises and have a smoother travel experience.

When planning your next adventure, consider up-and-coming destinations like Ljubljana and Medellín for their unique charm and evolving tourism landscape. Opt for LGBTQ+-friendly cities like Amsterdam and San Francisco to experience a welcoming atmosphere. Use tools such as Equaldex and consulate websites to learn about safety and legal issues, and always respect local customs to enhance your cultural experience. These tips will enhance your travel experience and promote an inclusive and respectful approach to the world.

Even if you don't consider yourself part of the LGBTQ+ community, it can still be helpful to familiarize yourself with the conditions in your destination country. A country's attitude towards LGBTQ+ rights can often be an indicator of overall tolerance and safety for minorities. This can allow conclusions to be drawn about how open and inclusive society is and how travelers, regardless of their origin, are treated locally. However, it should be noted that hospitality towards tourists can also depend on other factors, such as cultural norms and the economic situation.

This is How Sarah Would Approach It

After reading the first chapter on choosing the perfect destination, Sarah wants to try out the techniques and strategies described in the chapter when planning her next trip. As a busy corporate lawyer, she wants to ensure that the destination not only aligns with her personal interests but also takes into account important factors such as safety, budget and the environment. By implementing the chapter's recommendations, Sarah was able to systematically tackle her travel planning.

1. Assessment of Personal Interests and Preferences

The first thing Sarah did was think about her interests and the experiences she wanted on her trip. She loves the mix of relaxation and cultural insight but also looks for destinations that offer opportunities for outdoor activities and a sense of history. To narrow her choices, Sarah asked herself essential questions about the type of trip she envisioned. She considered whether she wanted to focus more on nature or explore the urban environment and whether cultural activities or outdoor adventures were more important to her.

After some thought, Sarah came up with three main areas that were decisive for her travel wishes: She wants to hike in scenic areas, explore cultural and historical sites and still have time to relax. These interests helped her choose potential destinations that would excite her and allow her to make the most of her free time.

2. Destinations on the Shortlist

Using the recommendations in this chapter, Sarah drew up a shortlist of possible destinations and began searching for places that would meet her needs. Ultimately, she narrowed her selection to five locations: Kyoto in Japan, Banff National Park in Canada, Lisbon in Portugal, Santorini in Greece and Medellín in Colombia. Each destination had something different to offer, but Sarah had to decide which one best suited her priorities.

Kyoto won them over with its perfect blend of culture and natural beauty, peaceful temples, ancient shrines and picturesque hiking trails. Banff beckoned with its pristine lakes and breathtaking landscapes offering endless hiking opportunities, but it didn't match her desire for a rich cultural experience. Lisbon, with its vibrant culture, historical sights and coastal atmosphere, was a wonderful place to explore Portugal's history and local traditions. Santorini, known for its iconic views and beautiful beaches, seemed more suited to a relaxing vacation, while Medellín intrigued her with its dynamic cultural boom and outdoor adventures. Each option was attractive, but Sarah had to make concrete considerations before deciding.

3. Assessment of Travel Restrictions and Safety

As described in the first chapter, Sarah next focused on assessing each shortlisted destination's safety and travel restrictions. She read the US State Department's travel advice and looked for additional information on the local authorities' websites.

Kyoto seemed to be a safe destination with high political stability and a low crime rate. Sarah noted that Japan has no special health requirements and that Kyoto's healthcare system is reliable. Lisbon also had a good safety rating and no major health concerns or travel restrictions. Sarah also made a note of the contact details of the respective embassies and local authorities in case of an emergency so that she could play it safe in the event of unexpected events on her trip.

4. Initial Budget Planning for Travel Destinations

Sarah needed to plan her budget when comparing the costs of traveling to each destination. The flights to Kyoto were longer and more expensive, and the total cost of accommodation and daily expenses in Japan was also higher. In contrast, Lisbon was more affordable, with cheap boutique hotels and cheaper local dining options.

When she compared the cost of activities, Kyoto's guided temple tours and cultural workshops, such as traditional tea ceremonies, were slightly more expensive. Still, Sarah appreciated the opportunity to immerse herself in Japanese traditions. In Lisbon, entrance fees for museums and walking tours were more budget-friendly. Sarah also found that she could save money by exploring the coastal areas or enjoying the local cuisine in inexpensive restaurants. Kyoto would require a higher budget, but its unique experiences aligned with Sarah's desire for more profound cultural and historical knowledge.

5. Using Technology and Apps to Plan Her Trip

The chapter highlights the importance of using digital tools for travel planning, and Sarah found this particularly useful when narrowing down her options. She used Instagram and Pinterest to get visual inspiration for Kyoto and Lisbon, using popular travel hashtags such as #KyotoTravel and #VisitLisbon. This helped her to see the destinations through the lens of other travelers and find out how well they matched her interests.

For the more practical aspects of her planning, Sarah used TripIt to compare possible flights and hotel bookings. This made it easy for her to compare prices and itineraries and determine which options best suited her schedule and budget. She also used Google Maps to check the proximity of critical attractions to the hotels she was considering, minimizing travel time between activities and making the most of her days on the ground.

6. The Decision Has Been Made: Kyoto in Japan

After weighing her personal interests, safety concerns and budget, Sarah finally decided on Kyoto as her next destination. Lisbon was more affordable and appealing, but Kyoto's rich cultural heritage, impressive temples and scenic hiking opportunities made it the perfect choice for her. By applying the structured approach from the first chapter, Sarah could confidently choose a destination that met her desire for adventure and relaxation.

During this planning process, Sarah found that the step-by-step approach described in the chapter works well. This helped her consider her interests, assess safety and travel logistics, and get an initial idea of her travel budget. The straightforward, practical approach enabled her to make an informed decision without feeling overwhelmed by too many options after her pre-selection.

Chapter 2: Determining the Duration of the Trip

Determining the ideal duration of your trip is a crucial aspect of travel planning to ensure that every moment you spend there is enjoyable and rewarding. Finding the right balance can be particularly difficult for busy professionals who want to reconcile their professional obligations with the desire to take time out. Travel enthusiasts also want to use their time efficiently to get the most out of their trip without feeling stressed or overwhelmed. Careful consideration of various factors can help determine the perfect length for a trip, whether it's a short trip or a more extended vacation.

In this chapter, you will learn practical strategies for determining the suitable duration for your trips. We should balance relaxation and discovery and ensure enough rest to keep our energy levels up throughout the journey. This chapter also includes practical tips on managing your workload in advance to avoid stress and disruption during your vacation. By taking into account important aspects such as travel time, possible delays and jet lag, you can significantly increase the enjoyment of your trip. This chapter also emphasizes the advantages of flexible working arrangements and the importance of clear boundaries between work and leisure. Using real-life examples and actionable advice, this chapter aims to equip travelers with the knowledge to plan balanced trips tailored to their needs and preferences.

Determine the Optimal Duration of the Trip

Determining the optimum travel duration depends heavily on the destination, the planned activities and the individual travel style. Different trips and destinations require different time frames to make the most of the journey without feeling stressed or missing out on meaningful experiences.

For city trips, 3 to 4 days are usually sufficient to visit the most important sights and get a good impression of the city. An example of this would be Paris. In 3 to 4 days, you can visit the Louvre Museum, see the Eiffel Tower and stroll through the charming Montmartre and Le Marais districts. Cities such as Barcelona or Berlin also offer numerous attractions that can be explored in just a few days without feeling rushed. A short but well-planned trip can offer much if you set your priorities right.

In contrast, cross-regional trips to distant countries or countries with great geographical diversity require significantly more time. For example, when you travel to New Zealand, a few days are often not enough to experience the country's diversity. At least two weeks are advisable to explore the North and South Island, hike in the national parks and get to know the Maori culture. Visiting Peru to hike the Inca Trail and Machu Picchu would also require a more extended trip, as acclimatization and exploring the capital, Lima alone can take several days.

For adventure and nature trips, such as trekking in the Himalayas or a safari in Kenya, you should also plan at least 10 to 14 days. Adventure travel often requires adapting to local conditions, whether reaching trekking camps, overcoming altitude differences or spotting wildlife in remote regions. In Nepal, the preparation for hikes near Mount Everest alone takes several days, and it would be a shame if you did not have enough time to acclimatize and enjoy the landscape in peace due to the short duration of your trip.

Another aspect is the combination of relaxation and discovery. For destinations by the beach or sea, such as the Maldives or Santorini, 5 to 7 days can be enough to combine relaxation with exploring the

27

surroundings. After a day at the beach, you can go on excursions to learn the local culture and history without feeling like you must do too much at once. This is often a reasonable duration for travelers looking for relaxation but still want to experience some activities.

Traveling with children requires special consideration of the duration of the trip. As traveling with children is often a little slower and breaks must be planned more frequently, allowing more time is advisable. For a family vacation in Europe, such as a visit to Rome or Vienna, 5 to 7 days might be suitable. This gives you enough time to explore the most important sights, but you can also take leisurely breaks or spend a day or two at the playground or in a family-friendly park. For more extensive trips, such as a family trip to Florida or Disneyland, you should plan at least a week to experience the theme parks and the surrounding attractions and relax.

Extending business trips to include a private vacation can also make sense to combine a professional stay with relaxation. For example, when traveling to New York for a conference, you can add 3 to 4 extra days to explore the city and see sights such as the Empire State Building, Central Park and the Statue of Liberty. Such short extensions can often be organized without much extra effort, and you make the most of the travel time available anyway. When traveling to more distant destinations, such as a business trip to Singapore, 5 to 7 extra days could be ideal for exploring the city and the surrounding islands while having enough time to relax.

Factor In Travel Time

When planning the duration of your trip, it is essential to consider the impact of travel time. Travel time can significantly impact your overall experience and efficiency.

First, consider the different means of transportation, including check-in times for flights and stopovers. Air travel often takes several hours, including security checks, boarding, and landing. In addition, stopovers can lead to further waiting times, which can add several hours or even half a day to the overall duration of your journey. If you have a stopover, for example, you can use the time to relax, eat something or explore what the airport offers so you do not get bored. Direct flights can make your schedule less complicated, although they may be more expensive.

Next, plan for possible delays and build buffer times into your itinerary. Due to weather conditions, technical problems or other unforeseen circumstances, delays must be expected. You can avoid the stress of missed connections or delays in your schedule by planning buffer times. For example, suppose you are attending a significant event or meeting shortly after your arrival. In that case, you should arrive the evening before to have enough time to prepare for any delays. If you book connecting flights or train journeys, you should allow extra time between connections to compensate for unexpected delays.

Another important aspect of travel planning is adapting your schedule to the time zone shift and dealing with jet lag. Jet lag occurs when your body's internal clock does not match the local time at your destination, leading to fatigue, insomnia and other symptoms. For each time zone you cross, you should allow 1-1.5 days for adjustment (Suni, 2021). Methods such as gradually changing your sleep pattern before departure, staying hydrated during the flight and exposing yourself to daylight after arrival can help mitigate the effects of jet lag. Bringing your bedtime and getting up the next day forward by one hour every two days can help you to adapt effectively and sustainably to the required conditions. This way, you can also try to align your meal and activity times with the local schedule right from the start during more extended stays.

Plan extra rest on arrival to recover from long flights and travel fatigue. Travel fatigue caused by hours of sitting, little sleep and changing environments can drain you. In contrast to jet lag, which affects your circadian rhythm, travel fatigue improves after a good night's sleep. When you arrive at your destination, you do not need to worry about your schedule. You can take time to rest and relax. This is particularly important if you have flown overnight or if significant turbulence has disturbed your sleep. Consider whether you want to spend your first day on a leisurely exploration tour or a spa treatment or get used to your new surroundings without overexerting yourself.

Strategies for Making the Best Possible Use of Limited Vacation Days

Efficient use of limited vacation days requires strategic planning so that you can enjoy your travels without feeling overly torn between work obligations and leisure. Instead of creating a perfect "work-life balance," you can take specific steps to get the most out of your free time while keeping your professional commitments in mind.

One proven strategy is to plan trips around holidays and weekends. This way, you can extend your vacation without using additional vacation days. For example, by taking a day around a holiday that falls on a Thursday or Tuesday, you can create a four-day weekend without putting a heavy strain on your vacation allotment. This method is precious for professionals with limited paid time off (PTO), as it allows you to maximize yoyr recovery and professional productivity.

Half-day trips offer another way to optimize your vacation. If you leave work early on Friday afternoon, you can start your trip that evening and gain almost a full extra vacation day without sacrificing a full vacation day. Returning from vacation can also be made more aceessible by taking a half day off, giving you time to recover before you dive back into your workday. This strategy minimizes the "vacation hangover" and sfmplifies kransktkoging back ko work.

Combining business and personal travel, often called "leisure," is a smart way to save money and extend trips. For example, if your company sends you to a conference or seminar in another city or country, you can schedule additional days off before or after the business portion. This allows you to explore new places without taking additional vacation days. This is especially useful if the company ayreasy covers part of the travel expenses. According to travel expert Sally French (NerdWallet), employees can also schedule business trips to include the weekend, thus combining professional and personal commitments without using their PTO.

Another aspect often underestimated when planning trips is choosing direct and early morning or late evening flights. Direct flights minimize the time in transit and maximize yeur time on site. For example, if you fly on Friday evening or Saturday morning, you can take advantage of the whole day at your destination without losing valuable vacation hours. This planning ensures you can maximize your time at your destination.

Taking advantage of holidays is also an effective way to extend your vacation. By cleverly planning bridge days, you can turn a few vacation days into more extended leisure. For example, you get an extended weekend if you take a day off around German Unity Day in October. Such "PTO hacks" can give you valuable time for longer trips without wasting your vacation.

31

Additionally, you can take advantage of the growing flexibility many companies offer through remote work. If your employer supports location-independent work, you can work while you travel and still spend more time at your destination. However, this flexibility requires that you have a stable internet connection and follow your employer's guidelines.

A well-planned itinerary is also crucial to mzgimizing your free time. Prioritizing your destinations and activities in advance will help you ensure that you make the most of your limited vacation days. Helpful technologies such as travel planning apps can help you organize your trip efficiently and keep track of all the details. We will discuss these tools in more detail later in the book.

Planning itineraries and being intentional about time zones are other ways to optimize travel time. By taking advantage of time zones, you can design your vacation to maximize your time in each location while facilitating the transition between work and leisure.

Balance Between Work and Vacation

For busy professionals and travel enthusiasts, balancing work commitments and vacation time is often a challenge. However, instead of assuming a rigid work-life balance that works for everyone, the key lies in consciously prioritizing and deciding when and how to focus on work or relaxation. Above all, your vacation should offer time out, and planning is crucial in how restful this time becomes.

First and foremost, consciously set aside time for relaxation and exploration. A vacation is not just a break from work but an opportunity to break out of your daily routine and recharge your batteries. The idea that you must balance everything perfectly often puts more pressure on you than it helps. Instead, the focus is on being in the moment – at work or on vacation. By scheduling downtime and keeping your itinerary light, you'll have the energy to make the most of your experiences.

One of the best ways to ensure uninterrupted relaxation is to delegate tasks and manage your workload before you leave. This will help to ensure that your professional obligations don't weigh you down during your travels. Setting clear deadlines and handing over open tasks to colleagues ensures that work continues uninterrupted in the office. This not only reduces the pressure on you but also empowers your team by giving them responsibility. If some tasks remain unfinished, it helps to set clear priorities – this way, you can be sure that urgent matters are taken care of in time and other tasks can wait when you return.

Talking to your employer about your vacation plans early on also helps set clear expectations and allows your team to prepare for your absence. It's not just about organizing the time of your absence but also about creating healthy expectations that you don't have to be constantly available during your vacation. This transparent communication ensures that your vacation is a time for rest without feeling like you must always be available.

In addition to planning your work, it is important to set aside specific time during your trip for activities that promote your mental and physical health. Activities such as hiking, swimming, or even just reading a book offer the opportunity to disconnect from the demands of everyday life. It is crucial to understand that there is no perfect balance – but rather a conscious decision to focus entirely on relaxation at certain moments.

Another critilal point is to free yourself from guilt when you take time off. Many professionals feel they are letting their colleagues

33

down or mtst "catch up" on work after their vacation. But the truth is that your rest will make you more productive in the long run. By letting go of these thoughts and thoroughly enjoying your vacation, you can approach your tasks with fresh energy and new motivation when you return.

Also, use modern technology to optimize your vacation and the preparation for it. Travel planning apps or productivity tools can help you keep track of things and ensure that you start your vacation well-organized. In later chapters, you will learn about other tools and technologies that will help you stay relaxed both before and during your trip.

Fulfilling Professional Obligations While Traveling

Balancing professional obligations with leisure time can often seem challenging. However, with the right preparation and conscious decisions, it is possible to find a sensible balance—without the pressure of having to balance everything perfectly. Some strategies can help busy professionals or self-employed people who want to enjoy their travel experiences while continuing to fulfill professional duties.

First of all, informing colleagues and clients about your travel plans well in advance is advisable. This enables your team to distribute tasks quickly and plan projects accordingly. Comgunicating your absence – for example, by leaving an out-of-office message – can help set realistic expectations. In this message, indicate when you will be available and whether there are alternative contacts for urgent matters. This step will help not only you but also your team to continue working smoothly.

A central element is setting clear boundaries. Instead of constantly checking work messages, you can set fixed times for dealing with emails and requests. These time slots could be, for example, 30 minutes a day during which you concentrate on work matters while the rest of the day is devoted to rest. These clear structures help you and show your team when and how you can be reached. This way, your free time remains undisturbed without affecting your workflow.

Modern technologies can also support this process. Cloud services and communication apps such as Slack or Microsoft Teams enable you to stay in touch with your team from anywhere without bging constantly online. You can access important documents, participate in meetings or delegate tasks from anywhere. Using project management tools such as Trello or Asana, you can keep track of ongoing projects without compromising travel. At the same time, status updates and communicated time slots ensure that your colleagues respect your working and vacation hours.

Negotiating flexible working arrangements can also help you balance work and leisure time. For example, if your employer allows it, you could work earlier to free up the afternoon for leisure activities. Alternatively, spreading your work across fewer days can help you enjoy long weekends or extended breaks. The important thing here is to communicate clearly with your employer and develop a plan that works for both sides.

If your trip crosses multiple time zones, make sure that you schedule your work hours to overlap with your home hours as much as possible. This will help keep communication efficient and allow you to separate your work and personal time better. Additionally, having a dedicated workspace at your destination can help you mentayly transition between work and rest. A café with Wi-Fi or a quiet corner in your hotel room can help you to work with focus without affecting your downtime.

It would be best ti remain consistent when colleagues or clients cross your work boundaries. Politely but firmly, you can remind them that you are unavailable outside your designated working hours and suggest a later time to process the requests. This encourages others to respect your boundaries and helps reduce misunderstandings in the long term.

A practical way to maintain control over your communication is to schedule emails in advance. The "send at a scheduled time" function allows you to ensure that messages are sent at the right time without being constantly active. This way, you can enjoy your free time undisturbed while your colleagues continue to receive the information they need.

Finally, it would be best to take regular time off to disconnect. While staying informed is important, it's essential to your mental and physical well-being to withdraw from work completely during certain periods. By consciously incorporating these breaks, you'll set yourself up to return to work with renewed energy and productivity after your trip.

This is How Sarah Would Approach It

After the first chapter, Sarah decided on Kyoto as her destination. She then used the strategies presented in the second chapter to determine the ideal duration of her trip. As a working lawyer with a busy schedule, she wanted to make sure her trip was both relaxing and enriching without feeling rushed or missing out on important experiences.

1. Determining the Optimal Duration of the Trip

As a first step, Sarah looked at the proposed criteria to determine the ideal duration of her trip to Kyoto. They aimed to experience both the city's cultural treasures and have enough time to explore the surrounding natural areas. As she already knew that Kyoto offered a wealth of temples, shrines and traditional gardens, she planned at least a week to enjoy the city and its surroundings at her leisure. The section in the chapter that combines relaxation and discovery was particularly relevant for Sarah. She wanted to combine exploration days in Kyoto with relaxing moments in nature, for example, on a trip to the surrounding mountains.

The examples in the chapter, such as the difference between city breaks and longer trips, helped Sarah find a good balance. She estimated that 7 to 10 days in Kyoto would be enough to discover the city and its surroundings without any time pressure. A trip of this duration would allow her to visit historic temples such as Kinkaku-ji and Fushimi Inari Shrine and have time for relaxing activities such as a walk through the tranquil gardens of Arashiyama Bamboo Forest.

2. Factoring In Travel Time

Another critical point in Sarah's planning was considering travel time, as discussed in the chapter. As Sarah would be traveling from Europe, she was aware that the flight to Japan and the time difference would significantly impact the duration of her trip. She planned the flight times carefully and preferred direct flights to avoid stopovers and unnecessary delays. The advice from the chapter to allow for buffer times was crucial here. Sarah decided to arrive in Kyoto a day before the planned start of her exploration to recover from the long journey and cope with possible jet lag.

The tips in the chapter on dealing with time zones and jet lag also helped Sarah strategically plan her adjustment to the local time in Japan. A few days before her departure, she wanted to slowly adjust her sleep rhythm to Japanese time by shifting her bedtimes forward by several hours. She also made a note to drink plenty of fluids during the flight, as recommended in the chapter, to reduce the effects of jet lag. After arriving, she would take it easy for the first few days to fully acclimatize before tackling the more intensive activities.

3. Strategies for Making the Best Possible Use of Limited Vacation Days

As Sarah only had limited vacation days available, she used the strategies presented in the chapter to plan them optimally. She decided to combine her trip with a national holiday to gain an extra day off without taking additional vacation days. This enabled her to go on a more extended trip without using too many precious vacation days.

The idea of combining business trips with leisure time was irrelevant for this trip, but Sarah noted this tip for future trips. However, the tips mentioned in the chapter, such as using bridge days and optimizing flight times, helped her make the most of her travel time. She opted for an early Saturday morning flight to spend the whole day in Japan and make the most of her first days of vacation.

4. Balancing Work and Vacation

Sarah wanted to relax during her trip entirely, but she also knew that she might need to check work emails in between. The tips from the chapter on setting clear boundaries between work and leisure time were constructive for them. She scheduled 60 minutes every morning to check emails before enjoying the rest of the day in peace. Setting these times in advance and letting her colleagues know when she would be available ensured that her work did not interfere with her travel.

Sarah also used the tools and technologies mentioned in the chapter to organize herself. She planned to use cloud services to access important documents in case urgent business matters arose during her trip. Using tools such as Slack and Google Drive, she could also ensure that she would remain reachable without being distracted by her trip.

5. Fulfilling Professional Obligations While Traveling

Finally, Sarah drew up a clear out-of-office note informing her colleagues and customers of her limited availability. She used the tips discussed in the chapter to manage professional expectations while ensuring she was disturbed as little as possible during her trip. She also planned to be available for emergencies, but only during the working hours she had agreed to, which would not restrict her free time too much.

Chapter 3: The Right Time for Your Trip: Best Seasons and Weather Patterns

Timing your trip to the best seasons and knowing the weather patterns can make a big difference to your trip. Whether you're busy at work and want to be efficient, or you love to travel and are looking for the best experience, this chapter will guide you through the ins and outs of choosing the perfect time to travel to different destinations. Knowing when to visit a place - depending on peak season, favorable weather conditions and cultural events - can make all the difference in ensuring you have as much fun and as little hassle as possible.

This chapter deals with essential aspects such as recognizing peak and off-seasons, understanding seasonal weather patterns, and planning cultural festivals. You will also learn how these factors affect costs, visitor numbers and the overall experience. It also provides practical tips on dealing with weather-related challenges and planning the timing of visits to key attractions to ensure a smooth and enjoyable trip. By the end of this chapter, you will be well-prepared to schedule your trips and ensure that each journey is as memorable and stress-free as possible.

Recognize High and Low Seasons

Knowing how the different seasons affect travel conditions and experiences is crucial for any traveler who wants to make their stay as enjoyable as possible while minimizing costs and stress. You can make informed decisions that match your travel goals by exploring your desired destination's high, low, and shoulder seasons.

Due to school vacations and public holidays, the high season is associated with higher costs and larger crowds. During this time, popular travel destinations are bustling and prices for flights, accommodation and sightseeing skyrocket. For example, flight prices soar during the Christmas or summer vacations, making traveling very expensive. In addition, the high demand often leads to fully booked hotels and long queues at the main tourist destinations. Cities such as Paris and New York are trendy during Christmas, as they are festively decorated and host famous holiday events. The dynamic atmosphere and well-organized events can be tempting, which means more people and higher costs.

On the other hand, traveling in the low season offers numerous advantages, including lower prices and fewer tourists. In mid-January, flights can be up to 50% cheaper than at Christmas. This savings opportunity also extends to accommodation, tours and entrance fees, making it a budget-friendly option. One example would be Rome in late fall when the temperatures are still mild, but the crowds are much smaller. With fewer people around you, you can enjoy a more relaxed workload and have better opportunities to interact with the locals to get an authentic insight into the culture and community of your destination. However, it is essential to inform yourself in advance, as some sights have restricted opening hours or are closed during this time.

The low season offers a balanced alternative with moderate costs and fewer crowds. During these periods, which lie between the high and low seasons, travelers can enjoy good weather and plenty of activities without having to deal with the crowds of the high season. Traveling in the low season can reduce your flight price by 23% on average. Cities like Kyoto or Barcelona are quieter in the low season, making securing reservations easier and avoiding long waits at popular attractions.

Another essential factor to consider when planning your trip is that the seasons are reversed in the northern and southern hemispheres.

41

For example, when it is warm in the European summer, it is winter in the southern hemisphere. This is vital in planning travel destinations in Australia, New Zealand, or Argentina, as the primary season is during the European winter months. While the European summer is a popular time to travel to the Mediterranean, destinations such as Cape Town or Buenos Aires offer pleasant temperatures and fewer crowds during the European winter. This allows you to take advantage of the summer months in the southern hemisphere and spend the winter in warmer climates.

Weighing up the advantages and disadvantages of the individual seasons helps you plan the best trip. Budget, tolerance for crowds and specific interests are crucial in determining the best time to travel. Off-peak travel is ideal for those who prefer cost savings and a quieter experience. Conversely, the high season could suit travelers who want to attend cultural festivals and events despite higher costs and larger crowds. In Japan, for example, the spring cherry blossom weeks are viral, attracting many tourists. The low season is a compromise that offers good weather and reasonable prices without the crowds getting out of hand.

Weather Conditions

Adjusting your travel plans to favorable weather conditions can significantly improve your travel experience. Knowing the best time to travel to a destination based on seasonal weather patterns is important, especially for outdoor activities.

There are rainy and dry seasons in many places, which can significantly impact the travel experience. In Thailand, for example, the summer months are the rainy season, which means regular, heavy rain showers. This time can still be attractive, as the country is green and less crowded with tourists. On the other hand, some countries have a transparent dry season, such as Ethiopia, where the weather is usually dry from October to April. During the dry season, outdoor activities such as hiking or safaris are ideal as the weather is stable and predictable. However, it is essential to be aware of the extreme temperatures during the dry season, which can be very high in some places.

However, some destinations offer a temperate climate all year round, such as Portugal or the Canary Islands, where temperatures remain mild, and both summer and winter are pleasant for travelers. Such places are ideal if you plan your trip flexibly without adapting to significant climatic fluctuations.

In other places, it rains almost all year round, such as in some regions of Scotland or Costa Rica. Being prepared for regular precipitation and taking appropriate clothing with you is essential. Nevertheless, these destinations offer fascinating experiences, especially for nature and adventure travelers who appreciate the beauty of the lush landscapes.

An excellent way to better understand the climate of a destination is to use climate charts. These charts show the average monthly temperatures and rainfall and give you an idea of what weather you can expect. You can find climate diagrams on websites such as Weather.com or Klimadiagramme.de. However, it is essential to emphasize that these diagrams only represent average values, which may differ from the actual weather conditions on-site. The temperatures on individual days can be significantly higher or lower than the climate diagram suggests. Especially in climate change, extreme weather events may occur more frequently than in the past.

In addition to climate charts, you can also view historical weather data for your destination to get a more accurate estimate of the time

Patrick Karban

of your planned stay. Websites such as Weather Underground or Climate Data offer historical weather records that can help you to estimate better whether it is more likely to be warm, cold or rainy during your travel time. This data can be a valuable addition to help you prepare for possible weather fluctuations.

Understanding weather patterns is essential for planning trips, especially for activities heavily dependent on certain conditions. For example, if you want to go skiing on the slopes, you must ensure enough snow. Conversely, plenty of sunshine and warm temperatures are essential if you dream of a beach vacation. By learning about the typical weather in the different seasons at your destination, you can make sure you find the right conditions for your favorite activities.

Even if the weather is often unpredictable in the low season, it offers unique and unforgettable experiences. If you travel at these times, you may encounter fewer tourists and benefit from lower prices. But this also means you must be prepared for everything, from sudden rain showers to unexpected cold snaps. This unpredictability can add a touch of adventure and spontaneity to your trip. If you open yourself up to possible surprises and remain flexible, you may discover aspects of the destination that many tourists miss.

The proper preparation with versatile clothing and equipment ensures comfort and safety, whatever the weather conditions. Layering clothing is essential, allowing you to adapt to different temperatures and conditions throughout the day. It is necessary to bring waterproof jackets, thermal clothing and sun protection. You can significantly improve your comfort with thoughtful clothing such as hats, gloves, and scarves for colder climates, swimwear, and lightweight jackets for warmer climates. The proper preparation in terms of clothing not only ensures that you feel comfortable but can also protect you from potential dangers such as hypothermia or heatstroke. Well-fitting footwear suitable for the activity is also essential, as uncomfortable shoes can quickly ruin a short hike or a stroll through town. We will go into this in more detail in the next chapter.

Planning for Weather-Related Challenges

Any experienced traveler must prepare well for the various weather conditions during the trip. By taking a few preparatory steps, you can ensure that you are prepared for whatever nature throws at you, making your trip safer and more enjoyable.

An essential strategy for dealing with changing weather conditions is regularly checking the weather forecast and using apps for real-time updates. If you keep an eye on the weather forecast, you can anticipate changes in the weather and plan accordingly. Several reliable weather apps provide up-to-date information on weather conditions worldwide. These include the Weather Channel app, Wetter.com, Windy.com and other local weather forecasting tools (US Department of Commerce, n.d.). If you keep yourself regularly updated with these apps, you can prevent your trip from being disrupted by sudden weather changes.

But even with the best planning, the weather can sometimes be unpredictable. Therefore, you must remain flexible in your travel plan and plan indoor activities as alternatives so that your trip remains fun even in bad weather. Planning visits to museums, aquariums, theaters and market halls can be rewarding and enlightening, offering cultural and educational experiences without depending on the weather. Flexibility in planning saves you from disappointment and enriches your travel experience with unique indoor activities that you might otherwise have missed.

Adhering to safety precautions for extreme weather situations is crucial to avoid potentially dangerous scenarios. Extreme weather conditions such as heat waves, hurricanes, snowstorms and avalanches require special safety measures. During a heatwave, you can prevent heat-related illnesses by drinking plenty of fluids, wearing light, protective clothing and postponing outdoor activities until the best time of day. Similarly, winter travelers need to know the signs of frostbite and hypothermia and how to stay warm and safe during snowstorms (Whitmore, n.d.). In addition, Imagine you are traveling to an area that is prone to hurricanes. In this case, it's essential to be aware of evacuation routes and plan if a storm arises where you are.

Travel safety apps can also improve preparation for adverse weather conditions. These apps can send you emergency warnings, inform you about road conditions and even connect you digitally with doctors if you need medical help. For example, suppose you pack a NOAA weather radio. In that case, you can receive emergency alerts near your current location and use them as a backup if your cell phone can't receive location-based weather alerts (U.S. Department of Commerce, n.d.).

If you plan a trip during tornado season, knowing the unique risks and safety precautions associated with tornadoes is essential. Tornadoes occur most frequently between March and July, especially in "Tornado Alley" in the Great Plains and the Midwestern United States (Whitmore, n.d.). Travelers should enable wireless emergency alerts on their phones to receive location-based alerts and check for updates from local weather services. In the event of a tornado, seeking shelter in a small, windowless room on the lowest floor of a sturdy building is advisable. For safety, it is essential to avoid places with large roofs, such as grocery stores or shopping centers, and to avoid underpasses that can create wind tunnel effects.

Those traveling during hurricane season should also be aware of the peak times, which usually occur on the Atlantic and Pacific coasts from June 1 to November 30. Staying in higher places, avoiding being near trees and finding out about your accommodation facility's rules on severe weather can save lives. If you are traveling by car, you should never drive through flooded streets, as the depth of the water can be deceiving and dangerous (Whitmore, n.d.).

Winter travelers must also be prepared for the rapidly changing conditions of winter storms. It is advisable to check the hourly weather data from the local weather service to avoid getting caught in a sudden snowstorm or whiteout. Winterizing your vehicle - winter tires, antifreeze and emergency equipment - can ensure a safe drive (US Department of Commerce, n.d.). Taking extra supplies such as food, water and warm layers of clothing with you is advisable, especially if you are stranded due to bad weather.

Availability of Places of Interest

Visiting attractions based on seasonal availability is critical to optimizing travel experiences. Knowing the peak and off-season periods will help you enjoy your trip even more, as you can ensure you get the most out of each destination.

In the high season, there are usually high occupancy rates and a comprehensive range of offers at the most important tourist destinations. This time often coincides with school vacations, public holidays and favorable weather conditions, attracting many people who want to explore famous sights. If you visit Paris in

47

summer, for example, you have full access to museums, parks and boat trips on the Seine. In addition, tourist services such as guided tours, restaurant opening hours and public transportation are usually extended to welcome more visitors.

However, the hustle and bustle of the high season also has disadvantages, such as long queues, overcrowded venues and higher prices for accommodation and entrance fees. However, the comprehensive experiences that many travelers have during these times outweigh the inconvenience. Disneyland, for example, operates all of its rides all year round and offers several entertainment shows throughout the day, providing a magical experience you can fully immerse yourself in. If you plan your visit during the high season, you can be sure that you will be able to experience all the essential sights and activities.

The low season, on the other hand, offers a different incentive. Even if you have to expect limited opening hours or even closures, there is a unique charm to experiencing a destination when it is quieter and more relaxed. Off-peak, there are fewer entertainment options and fewer staff at certain attractions. However, they also offer the opportunity to go on a discovery tour without the hustle and bustle of large crowds. Take Venice in late fall, for example. When most of the tourists are gone, you can enjoy a quiet gondola ride through the almost empty canals and get to know the beauty and culture of the city better.

Outside peak times, hotels, tour guides and restaurants are less busy, allowing for attentive and personalized service. They can help you with special requests, or tour guides can provide more detailed insights on a less hectic discovery tour. This level of attention can make your travel experience individual and unique.

It would be best to learn about opening times in advance to avoid the disappointment of discovering that your chosen attraction is closed or only open at certain times. Many destinations, especially those that depend on tourism, provide detailed information about seasonal operations on their websites. By planning well, you can ensure that your itinerary only includes the sights and activities available during your visit. For example, If you plan a trip to a national park, you must check whether the hiking trails or visitor centers are closed for maintenance work outside the primary tourist season. This helps to set realistic expectations and allows for alternative plans if necessary.

Another compelling reason for traveling off-season is the cost savings. As fewer tourists, flights, hotels, and some attractions can offer discounted prices. The financial benefits can be significant and allow you to spend your budget on other experiences or extend your trip. On the Greek islands, which usually teem with tourists in summer, there are considerable discounts on accommodation and ferry trips between May and October, for example. With this price cut, you can enjoy the same stunning beaches and ancient ruins at a fraction of the cost.

Seasonal festivals and events also play an important role in planning trips. They often coincide with the high season but can sometimes also take place in the low season. Participating in local festivals offers a deeper connection to the culture and traditions of the place you are visiting.

Imagine walking through the Louvre galleries and having the time to look at each work of art in peace without feeling rushed. Or enjoy a cozy meal in a renowned restaurant where the chef takes the time to talk to you about your dining experience. These quieter moments allow you to build a deeper connection with the destination and its people.

49

In addition, some attractions are designed to consider seasonality by offering special events outside peak times. According to Connell et al. (2015), many stores are open all year round but adapt their offer to attract visitors during quieter periods.

Cultural Festivals

To make your trip even more enjoyable, you should not only visit iconic sights or enjoy the local cuisine but also immerse yourself in the cultural diversity of your destination. Festivities and cultural events offer a unique perspective on the places you visit. This section will teach you how participating in these events can improve your travel experience.

Festivities often coincide with peak travel times and attract large crowds, making your trip livelier and more chaotic. Popular events such as the Rio Carnival in Brazil or the European Christmas markets attract tourists worldwide. In Venice, the carnival also occurs during the high season and attracts tourists with its spectacular masks and costumes. While these festivities offer an unparalleled insight into the local culture, they also bring the challenge of navigating crowded streets and dealing with inflated prices for accommodation and services. The atmosphere at these times is electric and full of music, parades, and communal celebrations, which make it worthwhile for many to endure the crowds anyway.

But not all festivities require you to fight your way through large crowds. Lesser-known festivities in the off-season offer equally rich cultural experiences without overwhelming crowds. These smaller events can be insider tips that provide a more robust social environment and a more relaxed atmosphere. One example is the Jinhae Cherry Blossom Festival in South Korea, which is less crowded than the famous festival in Tokyo but still offers spectacular cherry blossom landscapes. Visiting the Spring Festival in Beijing could also be a quieter alternative to the tourist highlights during the Chinese New Year celebrations. You can also visit local harvest festivals or art fairs, such as the Harvest Festival in Canada or the Venice Biennale, which promise a quieter yet enriching experience in the off-season. Participating in these intimate gatherings can create a natural and personal connection to the place and its inhabitants.

Find out in advance when these festivities are taking place so that you can experience these important cultural events. Websites dealing with tourism in certain countries often list the most essential festivals months in advance so you can plan accordingly. Travel apps and social media platforms can also help you learn about crucial festivals that coincide with your travel dates. You can tailor your itinerary to these cultural highlights if you know the dates for major events such as the carnival in Rio or the Christmas markets in Europe. This makes your trip even more exciting and allows you to participate in activities only available at this location.

For festivals in more remote regions, such as the Gnaoua World Music Festival in Morocco or the Cuzco Sun Festival Inti Raymi in Peru, you should plan well in advance. The infrastructure is often limited, and it can be difficult to find last-minute accommodation or transportation. Such festivals offer deep cultural insights but require careful preparation to ensure you get the most out of your visit.

Including cultural events in your travel plans will make your experience more intense and authentic. These events offer the opportunity to experience traditional dances or parades and learn more about the culture. For example, participate in workshops or tastings at a culinary festival such as the Oktoberfest in Munich.

You can try out traditional recipes and learn cooking techniques from the locals. At art festivals, such as the Edinburgh Festival Fringe, there are often live demonstrations where you can try to make items yourself under artisans' guidance. Such practical experiences leave lasting impressions and enrich your understanding of the local culture.

Policies like buying tickets to popular events in advance, showing up early to secure good seats, and familiarizing yourself with the schedule can significantly enhance your experience. Popular festivals often sell out quickly. So if you buy tickets as soon as they are available, you can secure all the benefits. If you arrive early, you'll avoid many crowds and have a better spot to enjoy the festivities. If you know the itinerary or program of the event, you can prioritize the activities you want to participate in and ensure you catch essential moments.

For those who want to escape the hustle and bustle of the big festivals, there are many smaller events off the beaten track that promise enriching experiences without the stress of moving through large crowds. Regional film festivals, niche food and drink exhibitions or local heritage days, such as the Heritage Day Festival in South Africa, offer fascinating insights into a community's traditions and modern life. These events are usually a mix of locals and travelers who enjoy exchanging ideas and learning from each other. Talking to the locals at these smaller gatherings can create memorable conversations and friendships that add another dimension to your travels.

This is How Sarah Would Approach It

Now that Sarah had decided to travel to Kyoto and had determined the duration of her trip in the second chapter, she turned her attention to the tips from Chapter 3. This chapter focused on choosing the best time to travel, considering seasons, weather conditions and cultural festivals. These factors were critical to Sarah as she wanted to make the most of her stay in Kyoto.

1. Recognizing High and Low Seasons

Sarah began by thinking about the best time to visit Kyoto. She knew Japan is particularly popular during the cherry blossom season in spring, making this a classic peak season. However, this also led to high visitor numbers and rising prices for flights and accommodation. Sarah was aware that Kyoto is particularly beautiful in spring, but she might also find it a crowded city.

However, the chapter also explained the advantages of the low season. Sarah wanted to avoid being surrounded by crowds of tourists and began to think about alternative times. As fall is also a popular time to travel in Japan but is less frequented by tourists than spring, Sarah decided to plan her trip for fall. Kyoto is a splendidly colorful city with pleasantly mild temperatures at this time of the year. Sarah had found the perfect balance: She could enjoy the beauty of nature while benefiting from moderate prices and a more relaxed atmosphere.

2. Taking Weather Conditions Into Account

Sarah also wondered how the weather would affect her activities in Kyoto. She planned to spend much time outdoors, visiting temples and gardens and hiking in the surrounding mountains. It was, therefore, vital for them to choose a travel time when the weather was ideal for such activities.

53

The chapter advised using climate charts and historical weather data to assess better what conditions to expect. Sarah researched and found that fall in Kyoto is relatively dry, with mild temperatures around 15 to 20 degrees Celsius. These conditions were perfect for their planned outdoor activities. She decided to take weatherproof clothing with her, especially a light rain jacket in case of showers, and several layers of clothing to be prepared for fluctuating temperatures throughout the day.

3. Planning for Weather-Related Challenges

Although Sarah planned her trip well, she knew the weather could be unpredictable, especially in a city like Kyoto, known for its changeable weather conditions. To be prepared for anything, she followed the advice in the chapter and installed the "Weather Channel" app on her cell phone to receive daily weather updates. This enabled them to adapt their activities accordingly and react quickly to sudden changes in the weather.

Sarah planned indoor alternatives in case the weather didn't cooperate. Kyoto offers numerous museums, including the Kyoto National Museum and traditional teahouses, which she could visit in bad weather. By being flexible with her itinerary, Sarah ensured that even rainy days would be exciting and educational.

4. Availability of Places of Interest

Another point Sarah considered was the seasonal availability of attractions. She wanted to ensure that all the important temples and shrines she wanted to visit were open during her stay. Thanks to the information in the chapter, she knew that many sights in Kyoto are open all year round. She researched the official websites of the most important attractions to learn about opening times and possible restrictions during her planned travel period.

One positive surprise was that fall in Kyoto attracts fewer visitors than spring so Sarah could experience some of the most famous temples, such as Kinkaku-ji and Fushimi Inari Shrine, in a quieter atmosphere. The fewer visitors also allowed her to book guided tours without long waiting times, and she looked forward to a more relaxed city tour.

5. Cultural Festivals

The chapter recommended including cultural festivals in travel plans to intensify the travel experience. Sarah had read that autumn in Kyoto is known for its many cultural festivals and temple ceremonies. She was particularly looking forward to the Jidai Matsuri, a traditional festival celebrated in Kyoto every October. It is one of Japan's largest historical festivals and offers Sarah the opportunity to immerse herself in the city's history and culture.

She planned to book tickets for the events in advance to ensure she would get a good seat and found out about the exact schedule of the festival in advance. The chapter advised finding out about the most important festivals well in advance, and thanks to these tips, Sarah was able to plan her stay around this special event.

Chapter 4: Booking Flights and Means of Transportation

Booking flights and transportation is essential for planning any long-haul trip, whether you're traveling for business or pleasure. Your choices can significantly impact your budget, your comfort and your environmental footprint. Every decision, from choosing the right airline to selecting local transportation, plays a crucial role in shaping your travel experience. This chapter looks at various strategies that professionals and travel enthusiasts can use to manage the complexities of booking flights and organizing transportation.

In this chapter, you will learn how to find the best flight deals using various effective methods. This includes using flight comparison sites, setting up price alerts and taking early booking and last-minute offers into account. The chapter also deals with the advantages and disadvantages of alternative airports and routes. It also states that you should use several comparison tools to stay informed about price trends. It also explains the importance of understanding airline policies and fees to avoid unexpected expenses. Finally, tips on using sustainable modes of transportation such as public transport, ridesharing and cycling are discussed to ensure an environmentally friendly journey. With these strategies, you can realize a more efficient, cost-effective and sustainable journey.

Find the Best Flight Deals

Many travelers are looking for affordable airfares. This is especially true for busy professionals and travel enthusiasts who want to enhance their travel experience at the lowest possible cost.

Various strategies exist for this, all of which, if used effectively, lead to significant cost savings.

One of the most reliable ways to find cheap prices is to use flight comparison sites such as Skyscanner and Kayak. These platforms combine data from several airlines and travel agencies and offer a comprehensive overview of available flights. You can compare the options by entering your starting point, destination and travel dates. This approach saves time and ensures you get the most for your money.

You should consider early bookings and last-minute offers to make your search easier. Prices are often lower for early bookings because the airlines want to fill the seats sooner rather than later. For example, buying tickets several months in advance usually saves costs. However, last-minute deals can offer significant discounts, especially when airlines try to sell unsold seats. You must be flexible with your travel dates and destinations to take advantage of these opportunities.

The use of alternative airports and routes can also lead to cost reductions. In large cities, there are often several airports; if you fly from a second airport, you may be able to get cheaper fares. For example, if you fly to Oakland instead of San Francisco or Newark instead of JFK, you can sometimes save a lot of money. You can also reduce costs by considering flights with stopovers instead of direct flights. These alternatives are not always convenient but can significantly reduce travel costs.

Using fare alerts and filters on comparison sites such as Skyscanner and Kayak will keep you informed of price changes so that you don't miss out on any offers. Once you have found potential flights, you can set up price alerts. This function notifies you by e-mail or app if the price for the selected route changes. By being proactive with price alerts, you can book at the lowest possible rate and increase your chances of getting a better deal.

You can get a better overview of price trends by including several comparison tools in your research. In addition to Skyscanner and Kayak, Google Flights offers an intuitive platform for tracking flight prices. It allows users to see the price history of certain flights and determine whether the prices for the selected route are currently average, high or low. Google Flights' price graph and date grid visually represent price fluctuations over time to help with booking decisions. (How to Use Flight Price Alerts to Save Money on Your Next Trip, n.d.)

Another valuable tool is Momondo, which is less well-known in the US but is very influential for international flight searches. Momondo's "Flight Insights" provides detailed reports on the cheapest flight times, including the most affordable months, days of the week and airlines. If you set up price alerts via Momondo, you will stay updated on all fluctuations.

An important strategy for securing cheap airfare is to remain adaptable. If you travel in the middle of the week, for example, you can often get cheaper tickets than at the weekend. Prices are generally higher on public holidays and during peak travel times, so you can make considerable savings when planning trips at off-peak times.

Understanding and using these different methods will increase your chances of finding cheap flights and make travel planning smoother and less stressful. Implementing these strategies requires minimal effort but can significantly impact your travel budget.

Watching seasonal offers and special promotions is also advantageous when considering early bookings and last-minute offers. Airlines often organize discount promotions that significantly reduce ticket prices. If you subscribe to an airline's newsletter and follow it on social media, you can learn about these limited-time offers. Participating in frequent flyer programs is also beneficial, as members often receive exclusive access to sales and special offers that are not available to the general public.

When saving on airfare, make sure that the additional cost or time associated with a longer journey from the alternative airport to your destination is outweighed by the savings. Inquire about transportation options from these secondary airports and look for affordable shuttles or public transportation that will quickly get you to your primary destination.

Price alerts and filters on comparison sites provide real-time updates so you can seize the moment when prices drop. At Kayak, for example, you can set up flexible date alerts that inform you of the lowest prices within a specific time frame. This flexibility benefits those who plan their vacation according to the best offers rather than fixed dates. According to Lindsay from Skyscanner, enabling multiple price alerts for different airports and dates expands your options and increases your chances of finding a good deal. (How to Use Flight Price Alerts to Save Money on Your Next Trip, n.d.)

It's worth noting that while technology offers convenience, traditional methods should not be disregarded entirely. If you go to a travel agency for advice, you can sometimes find hidden offers that cannot be found online. They have industry knowledge and access to exclusive offers that individual consumers may not get. Combining modern and traditional methods gives you the best chance of getting the best rate.

Understanding Airline Policies and Fees

Knowing airline policies to avoid unnecessary expenses is essential for every traveler, especially busy professionals and travel enthusiasts who want to experience as much as possible and keep planning stress to a minimum. By knowing the ins and outs of the various airline policies, you can significantly reduce unexpected costs and ensure a smooth journey.

One of the most critical areas is understanding the baggage policy. Airlines have different guidelines for hand and checked baggage, which can lead to unexpected costs if you don't know them exactly. For most airlines, hand baggage may only exceed specific dimensions and weights. For example, many European airlines allow hand baggage dimensions of 22 x 16 x 8 inches or 22 x 18 x 10 inches, while the weight restrictions are often 14 to 20 pounds. Ryanair or Wizz Air offer cheap tickets but usually require more oversized items of hand baggage or additional baggage to be booked at an extra charge. At EasyJet, hand baggage may be carried without weight restriction as long as it corresponds to 22 x 18 x 10 inches dimensions.

Similar variations apply to checked baggage. The usual weight limits for checked baggage are between 30 and 46 pounds, although Ryanair offers a checked baggage allowance of 40 pounds for around $20 to $30 if booked in advance. Lufthansa's weight limit for an Economy ticket is 46 pounds, but exceeding this limit can lead to fees of up to $100 or more, depending on the flight route and the excess weight.

Another critical area is the guidelines for flight changes and cancellations. Your plans may change, and you may have to adjust your itinerary. Different airlines have different policies for rebooking and canceling, ranging from flexible adjustments to nonrefundable tickets. For example, the US Department of Transportation has issued regulations requiring airlines and ticket agencies to disclose these fees in advance. This transparency lets travelers make accurate decisions before booking (Final Rule - Enhancing Transparency of Airline Ancillary Service Fees | US Department of Transportation, 2024). Therefore, always check the airline's change and cancellation policy to determine the possible costs of changing your travel plans. Some airlines offer free rebooking within a certain period, while others may charge considerable fees.

Looking for additional services and upgrade options is another strategy to improve your trip while managing costs effectively. Additional services include options such as seat selection, priority boarding, seats with extra legroom and in-flight meals. These offers can make your journey more comfortable and convenient but also involve additional costs. Ryanair charges around $ 8 to $15 for priority boarding, allowing you to carry a larger piece of hand baggage. EasyJet seats with extra legroom cost between $ 12 and $ 25 each way, which can be worthwhile on longer flights. An upgrade to Premium Economy with airlines such as British Airways costs between $ 200 and $ 400, depending on availability, and offers more legroom and additional services.

Prepaying for checked baggage and taking advantage of credit card benefits are practical strategies to minimize costs. Many airlines offer discounts if you pay for your checked luggage and not at the airport during the booking process. For example, a 46-pound piece of checked baggage with EasyJet costs around $ 20 to $ 35 if booked online in advance, while the price at the airport can go up to $ 50. Credit cards such as the American Express Platinum offer benefits such as free checked baggage, faster boarding or up to $

61

100 travel credit, which can bring you considerable savings. If your card offers these benefits, use them when booking.

Comparison of Transportation Options at the Destination

An efficient transportation choice can significantly improve the travel experience, especially for busy professionals and avid travelers. Whether you want to save money, help the environment or improve comfort, choosing the suitable mode of transportation locally can make a big difference. The following four methods each have their advantages and potential disadvantages.

Public transportation is still one of the most cost-effective and environmentally friendly travel methods. Buses, streetcars and trains generally offer lower fares than private vehicles or ridesharing services, which makes them very economical. In addition, public transportation systems typically have an extensive network that covers large urban areas and ensures accessibility. For example, in cities like New York, London, or Tokyo, their mass transit systems can take you almost anywhere without dealing with traffic or finding parking.

Another advantage of public transportation is special tourist tickets, which are offered in many cities. In Ireland, for example, there is a regional ticket for the Dublin region that tourists can purchase for $16. This ticket allows unlimited travel on all public transport for three days. In comparison, a train journey from Dublin to a nearby city costs $5 for both trips and bus travel within Dublin is omitted. Such regional tickets can save considerable costs, especially if you are spending several days in one region.

Public transportation is not only good for your wallet but also an environmentally friendly alternative. By using buses or trains, you help to reduce the number of cars on the roads, which lowers overall carbon emissions and reduces traffic congestion. Buses often use high-occupancy vehicle lanes, making them faster than a car, especially at peak times. However, the convenience of public transport can be limited by various factors, such as overcrowded spaces or irregular timetables.

For those who value comfort and convenience, private transfers such as cabs or chauffeur-driven cars offer a better experience, albeit at a higher cost. These services pick you up from your desired location and drop you off at your destination, so you don't have to change or wait several times. Private transfers can be especially beneficial for business travelers who need to increase productivity and minimize downtime between meetings. Plus, traveling in a private vehicle offers more privacy and comfort, whether checking emails, preparing for a meeting or simply relaxing.

The disadvantage is that private transfers can quickly become expensive, especially for longer distances or frequent travel. The costs include the fares and possible additional costs such as tolls. In many rental cars, toll devices can be easily activated, and the toll will be charged to your credit card after the trip. This comfort can be an advantage on longer journeys but does not permanently save money. Please note that many car rental providers block up to $250 as a deposit on your credit card. You must ensure that this amount remains available to avoid complications.

Ridesharing services like Uber and Lyft offer a balance between the affordability of public transportation and the convenience of private transfers. With the help of mobile apps, these services provide real-time tracking, transparent prices and often lower prices than conventional cabs (Carsharing to Help Save the Planet | Green City Times, 2017). This makes ridesharing an excellent middle ground for many travelers. In addition, simple payment via mobile apps and sharing journeys with other passengers further reduce costs and contribute to environmental sustainability.

Renting vehicles or bicycles offers even more flexibility and independence. A rental car can be exciting for travelers planning day trips to remote or rural areas that are difficult to reach by public transport. However, taking out fully comprehensive insurance would be best to avoid unexpected costs. In many cases, fully comprehensive insurance covers damage to the rental car, while other insurance policies may only cover part. It is also essential to check the terms of the rental contract carefully, as additional insurance may be offered locally. Sometimes, these are already included in your insurance, or you can even cancel existing insurance - so clarify this to avoid double costs.

In unfamiliar surroundings, minor accidents can happen quickly, even if you are an experienced driver, so fully comprehensive insurance significantly reduces costs. In the case of rental car contracts, damage that exceeds average consumption can quickly result in the often-agreed excess of $ 2,500 being claimed. This will then be reimbursed afterward by fully comprehensive insurance. As many rental companies abroad only accept credit cards, you should also ensure that the excess specified in the contract can be covered in an extreme emergency.

Bicycles are an excellent alternative in urban centers as they produce no emissions and promote health through physical activity. Many cities now have bike-sharing programs where you can rent bikes for short periods. This allows you to navigate the crowded city streets and avoid traffic jams. By bike, you can experience the city from a different perspective, discover hidden gems and appreciate your surroundings in a way that is difficult to do in a car.

Public transportation is ideal for budget-conscious and environmentally-conscious travelers but may not offer the flexibility needed for specific itineraries. Private transfers provide unparalleled comfort and convenience at a premium price and are therefore suitable for those willing to invest for a smooth ride. Ridesharing services offer a balanced approach that combines moderate costs with great convenience and flexibility. Renting vehicles or bicycles affords you the greatest possible freedom but entails several financial and logistical considerations.

Depending on your destination, it can be advantageous to combine different modes of transportation to get the most out of your trip. On a trip to Dublin, for example, it can make sense to hire a car to drive from the airport to your accommodation. It is worth asking the operator of your accommodation if there is a train station nearby that is less frequent and still offers a fast connection to the city center. It is often easier and cheaper within the city to use public transport such as buses or streetcars. At the same time, you can keep the rental car ready for day trips into the surrounding countryside to enjoy the flexibility for more distant destinations.

Using Sustainable Transportation Options

Choosing environmentally friendly transportation methods is an essential step towards sustainable travel. This approach helps the environment and enhances the travel experience by offering unique perspectives and improved health benefits.

One of the most environmentally friendly transportation options is traveling by train. Trains emit significantly less carbon emissions than airplanes or cars, making them an excellent choice for long-distance travel. According to recent studies, trains can emit between 70 and 80 % less greenhouse gases than other modes of transport

(Pei, 2021). In addition, the travel experience is enhanced by the picturesque views that a train journey offers. For example, routes such as the Trans-Siberian Railway or the Rocky Mountaineer offer breathtaking landscapes that are often missed when traveling by air.

Modern buses are another excellent option for shorter distances. These buses have been designed to be both cost-effective and environmentally friendly. They use advanced technologies to reduce fuel consumption and emissions. Riding a modern bus can significantly reduce CO_2 emissions compared to driving a private vehicle. Buses are particularly beneficial in urban areas as they help to reduce traffic congestion and air pollution. Not only are they a more environmentally friendly alternative, but they are also affordable and, therefore, accessible to a broader audience.

Car-sharing and ride-sharing services such as Zipcar and BlaBlaCar significantly reduce the number of road vehicles. With these services, people share a single vehicle for their journey, so fewer cars are needed to transport the same number of people. This lower number of vehicles leads to fewer emissions and less congestion. In addition, ridesharing services often use newer vehicle models that comply with stricter emission standards, further contributing to environmental protection. Car sharing also promotes efficient use of resources, as users only pay for the time they need the car, thus avoiding unnecessary vehicle costs.

Bicycles are the ideal solution for anyone who prefers a more active way of getting around. Cycling causes no emissions and offers numerous health benefits. It is particularly effective in cities, where you can navigate through narrow streets and reach places inaccessible to larger vehicles. Cycling improves cardiovascular fitness, increases mental well-being and reduces stress levels. In many cities, the infrastructure for cyclists is being expanded, e.g., through dedicated cycle paths and rental services, making it easier for travelers to opt for this environmentally friendly mode of transport.

Incorporating environmentally friendly means of transportation into travel planning requires a shift in awareness from convenience to sustainability. Even if it initially seems challenging, the benefits far outweigh the effort. By choosing the train over the plane, the bus over the car and the bike over the cab, you contribute to a cleaner environment. This can save money in the long run.

Busy professionals who want to improve their travel experience can integrate eco-friendly practices to achieve global sustainability goals and enhance their personal growth and awareness. Sustainable travel offers the opportunity to build a deeper connection with destinations and the locals. For example, a bike tour through a city's historic districts provides a deeper understanding of the local culture than a trip by car. They shared a car with locals while carpooling, leading to interesting conversations and insights you might otherwise miss.

Furthermore, the economic benefits of sustainable transport must not be ignored. Public transportation, such as buses and trains, often costs only a fraction of the cost of private rental cars or flights. With these options, travelers can spend their budget on experiences and activities instead of expensive transportation costs. In addition, many cities offer discounts and incentives for using public transportation, reducing the financial burden on travelers.

On a larger scale, supporting sustainable transport initiatives encourages governments and organizations to invest more in green infrastructure. When demand for environmentally friendly options increases, innovation and development in this sector will increase, and improved public transport networks, better cycle paths, and

67

expanded car-sharing schemes could become the norm, benefiting travelers and the local population.

Careful planning is required to integrate these environmentally friendly methods seamlessly. You can start by researching the options available at your destination. Many cities offer detailed guides to public transportation, bike rentals and car-sharing services. Apps and websites dedicated to sustainable travel can help you find the best options for your itinerary. You should also pack light to get around quickly, whether on a train or bus or cycling through the streets.

For companies that organize business travel, green transport can also be aligned with corporate social responsibility (CSR) goals. Encouraging your employees to use sustainable transportation demonstrates your commitment to the environment. It promotes a culture of health and well-being within the company. Incentives such as subsidized tickets for public transport or the use of company bicycles can motivate employees to make more environmentally friendly decisions.

Ultimately, the goal of introducing environmentally friendly transportation methods goes beyond individual benefits. It is about contributing to a collective effort to preserve our planet for future generations. Every decision, no matter how small, whether you choose the train over the plane, share a ride instead of driving alone, or ride your bike through the city, has a significant positive impact.

Use Loyalty Programs and Frequent Flyer Miles

Enhancing travel benefits through loyalty programs is essential for busy professionals and travel enthusiasts who want to get the most out of their trips. Concentrating on the most critical aspects, you can collect points quickly, achieve elite status and redeem rewards in the best possible way. In this section, you will find practical tips and strategies to help you optimize your travel experience with loyalty programs.

One effective way to improve travel rewards is to focus on one or two loyalty programs. If you bundle your activities, you can collect points more efficiently. For example, if you fly frequently with Lufthansa and regularly stay at Marriott hotels, participating in their Miles & More and Bonvoy loyalty programs can bring significant benefits. Frequent flyers who regularly travel with a particular airline often find that they can get upgrades, free flights or lounges more quickly by using a specific program. Choose programs that suit your travel habits and destinations, whether you are traveling for business or pleasure.

Using travel credit cards specifically designed for earning travel points can further shorten your path to elite status. Many of these cards offer sign-up bonuses that can earn you significant points if you meet the minimum spend within a few months. For example, the Chase Sapphire Preferred® often offers 60,000 points as a sign-up bonus when you spend $ 4,000 within the first three months. These cards often offer more points per euro spent on travel-related bookings such as flights, hotels and restaurants. Cards like the Platinum Card® from American Express also offer access to lounges and travel credits, which can significantly enhance your travel experience. When choosing a travel credit card, you should consider factors such as annual fees, points multipliers for everyday spending and additional perks that increase the value of your card.

If you achieve elite status in a loyalty program, you can enjoy numerous benefits, such as room upgrades, priority boarding and access to exclusive lounges. With Delta SkyMiles, for example, Diamond Medallion members receive up to 125% more miles per flight. These benefits improve your travel comfort and speed up the collection of points. A room upgrade at a hotel chain like Hilton Honors can transform your stay from a standard room to a suite at no additional cost. Elite members also often receive bonus points for every flight or hotel stay, making their loyalty program participation even more valuable.

Strategically redeeming points is crucial to getting the most out of your loyalty programs, especially during peak travel times with high prices. Redeeming Miles & More miles for flights to New York or Singapore during the summer vacation or Christmas season can significantly increase the value of your points. Instead of redeeming points for less valuable rewards like merchandise, you can use them for flights or hotel stays when prices are at their highest. Some programs also offer bonuses if the points are redeemed via specific portals. For example, the Chase Sapphire Preferred® provides 25% more value when points are used for travel bookings through the Chase Ultimate Rewards portal, meaning your points are worth more on travel than other spending.

In addition to using points for basic travel expenses, you should also take advantage of special promotions and bonus categories to better use your benefits. Some credit cards, such as the American Express Gold Card, offer triple points for restaurant visits and flight bookings, which can quickly add up. Also, watch for limited-time bonus promotions, such as extra points for car rental bookings or gas during vacation periods. These can significantly increase the value of your rewards and bring you additional savings.

Participating in online shopping portals linked to your travel credit cards can also help you increase your rewards. On portals like Delta Air Lines SkyMiles Shopping or Shop Through Chase, you can earn additional points on top of your regular credit card rewards when you shop through them. For example, you could earn up to x5 points when buying electronics on these platforms, allowing your miles to increase faster. For those whose credit cards don't have their web portal, third-party websites like Rakuten offer cashback to help you make additional savings.

An advanced strategy for seasoned travelers is to use multiple credit cards to take advantage of the various rewards programs. For example, you could use the Chase Sapphire Reserve® for restaurant visits, the Amex Platinum for hotel bookings and the Capital One Venture Rewards for flights. While this approach requires careful management to thoroughly utilize each card's minimum spend and benefits, it maximizes the point's potential. But always keep an eye on the annual fees and your total expenditure.

Combining points and cash can lead to considerable savings and better use of your points. This strategy is beneficial during peak travel times when spending all your points on a booking is not worth spending. For example, if you pay 50% of your travel expenses in cash and the remaining 50% in points, you can optimize the value of your points and reduce your budget simultaneously. This hybrid form is ideal for both collecting points and remaining flexible.

This is How Sarah Would Approach It

Now that Sarah had decided on the time and duration of her week-long trip to Kyoto, she turned her attention to the next important task: booking flights and transportation. Based on the strategies from Chapter 4, she used a systematic approach to find the best

71

airfares and plan the most sensible means of transportation in Kyoto.

1. Finding the Best Flight Deals

First, Sarah set about finding the best flights to Japan. Being flexible with her travel dates, she used flight comparison sites such as Skyscanner and Google Flights to compare prices for different periods. Thanks to the strategy described in the chapter, it set up price alerts to inform them of changes in flight prices. This function enabled her to react to price reductions at any time and choose the best time to book.

Using Google Flights was beneficial, as it gave her a clear overview by graphing the price fluctuations. This allowed Sarah to determine the best time to travel and ensure she didn't have to overpay for her flight. As she booked several months in advance, she benefited from lower prices, as early bookers usually get better deals.

Sarah found that direct flights from her home airport to Osaka, the closest international airport to Kyoto, were more expensive than flights with a stopover in Tokyo. She could reduce her travel costs considerably by choosing the option with a stopover, even if the journey took a little longer. This flexibility saved her around $ 200.

2. Understanding the Airline's Flight Policies and Fees

While Sarah was comparing flights, she also made sure to check the policies and fees of the different airlines to avoid any unpleasant surprises. Thanks to the information in the chapter, she ensured she was fully aware of the baggage regulations for hand and checked baggage. She opted for an airline with checked baggage in economy class, as she wanted to travel with a medium-sized suitcase. She ensured that the permitted weight of 46 pounds was not exceeded to avoid additional charges.

The airline's cancellation and rebooking policies were also crucial for Sarah. As plans are always subject to change, she opted for a fare that allowed her to rebook the flight for a small fee if necessary. This flexibility gave her security without having to take unnecessary risks.

3. Comparing Transportation Options at Her Destination

Another critical step in Sarah's travel planning was organizing the means of transport on site. She decided to take the train because she had to travel to Kyoto after arriving in Osaka. The Shinkansen, the express train, connects Osaka with Kyoto in only about 15 minutes, the most comfortable and fastest option. As train transportation in Japan is very efficient, Sarah planned to use the public transport network for most of her trips in and around Kyoto.

Sarah opted for a tourist ticket for public transportation in Kyoto, which allowed her unlimited travel by bus and train during her stay. This was cost-effective and environmentally friendly, as she minimized CO_2 emissions by avoiding cabs and rental cars.

However, as she also plans to take a few day trips to more rural areas around Kyoto, she decided to rent a car for two days. To keep costs low, she booked the rental car in advance and chose fully comprehensive insurance to be covered in the event of damage. She ensured that the credit card she used to book the rental vehicle already included insurance, which saved additional costs.

4. Using Sustainable Transportation Options

Patrick Karban

Following the tips in the chapter, Sarah also wanted to make environmentally friendly choices during her trip. In addition to public transportation, she planned to use Kyoto's bike rental services, which offer a sustainable and healthy way to explore the city. As Kyoto is a relatively flat city with many cycle paths, this was an ideal way for Sarah to discover both the temples and the city's picturesque gardens in an environmentally friendly way.

5. Using Loyalty Programs and Frequent Flyer Miles

As Sarah travels regularly, she also decided to use frequent flyer programs and credit card points to get the most out of her bookings. She already had a credit card that earned miles with her favorite airline, and by booking her flight, she could earn additional miles. She would later redeem these for an upgrade or future flights. She also used a travel credit card that offered bonus points for her flight and hotel bookings, allowing her to collect further benefits.

Chapter 5: Basic Packing Tips for a Stress-Free Trip

Efficient packing is crucial for a stress-free travel experience. Whether planning a weekend getaway or preparing for a business trip, knowing what to pack can make all the difference. Packing too much leads to unnecessary stress and bulky luggage, while with too little luggage, you are not prepared for various situations. A strategic approach to packing ensures that you can take everything you need without overloading yourself with unnecessary items.

This chapter contains practical tips and strategies tailored to different types of travel, such as weekend getaways and business trips. You will learn to create versatile packing lists for specific activities and environments, such as outdoor adventures or urban exploration. If you focus on multifunctional items and know the local customs and weather conditions, you will be prepared for any challenges that come your way. In addition, techniques for organizing and compressing your luggage ensure that you have as much space as possible and that everything remains accessible and orderly so that your journey is smooth and enjoyable from start to finish.

Create a Versatile Packing List

Optimizing your travel preparations also goes hand in hand with one of the most critical tasks: organized packing. A structured approach ensures you have everything you need without overloading yourself with unnecessary items. Adapting your packing list to different travel situations, such as weekend getaways or business trips, is essential to be efficient and well-prepared.

Of course, a more specific packing list is required for business trips. In addition to clothing, you also need to pack essential things for work, e.g., a laptop, chargers and necessary documents. Opt for wrinkle-resistant clothing that looks professional straight out of the suitcase. Packing cubes allow you to separate your business and casual clothes neatly. A small first aid kit and travel-sized toiletries will save you time when you need these items between meetings and events.

Multifunctional items play an essential role in both types of travel. Pants can be converted into shorts or jackets with a removable inner lining that adapts to changing environments and activities. If you invest in items that serve multiple purposes, you will have to pack fewer things and can save valuable space. Shoes that you can also wear as casual wear can reduce the number of shoes that are often the clunkiest part of your luggage.

Another strategy to improve your ability to travel is to pack activity-specific items. If you are planning outdoor activities such as hiking or swimming, pack the right equipment for these activities. For example, hiking boots, moisture-repellent clothing and a light jacket are essential for a hiking tour. On a beach vacation, you should prefer swimwear, flip-flops and sunscreen if you do not want to buy them locally.

Weather-appropriate packing includes quick-drying clothing for humid environments, thermal clothing for colder regions and UV-protective clothing for sunny destinations. If the weather is unpredictable, you can adapt quickly by packing several layers. Lightweight jackets, sweaters and scarves can significantly increase comfort without taking up too much space.

Packing lists that are tailored to cultural expectations are just as important. Visiting religious sites may require modest clothing;

packing long sleeves and pants provides flexibility. You can quickly adapt your outfit with versatile scarves or shawls to any local norm. For countries with different standards for formal and informal occasions, it is helpful to bring adaptable clothing. A blazer, for example, can enhance an otherwise casual outfit for a formal dinner or meeting.

After all, you should always leave some free space in your luggage. This space is invaluable for souvenirs or items you buy during your trip. Packing leaves little room for extra items and can lead to stress when closing an overstuffed suitcase. Repacking techniques, such as compressing bulky items and regularly checking your luggage's contents, help keep things tidy and save space.

Frequent repacking also ensures that you only take the essentials with you. If you put your things on a table every few days, you will recognize what is essential and what is dispensable. Compression bags save space by reducing the volume of items such as sweaters and jackets. Pack essential items such as travel documents and a small first aid kit in easily accessible compartments so that you can access them quickly if necessary.

Choosing the Right Type and Size of Luggage

Choosing the right luggage is crucial for a stress-free and efficient travel experience. The first step is to assess the duration and activities of the trip to make a sensible decision. A weekend trip requires different packing methods than a two-week vacation or a business trip with meetings and evening events. Short trips are often best managed with hand luggage, which saves time at the check-in counter and helps avoid checked baggage fees (Wheeler, 2023). In this way, travelers can avoid long waiting times at baggage reclaim and continue their journey to their next destination immediately after arrival.

For a weekend getaway, you should focus on things that make traveling light easier. A small travel bag or a compact backpack should suffice. Your packing list could include two versatile outfits that can be combined in any way you like. You can also pack a pair of hiking boots and a manageable selection of toiletries.

If you keep it simple, you can manage short trips without heavy luggage. For example, we have the 5-4-3-2-1 packing method: five tops, four bottoms, three pairs of shoes, two layers and one smart garment. This method offers enough variety for a week's travel and is also very space-saving.

For more extended stays or trips with different activities - from hikes to festive dinners - luggage with expandable compartments is invaluable. If required, these compartments offer additional space without passengers being forced to carry oversized luggage items from the outset. This flexibility is particularly advantageous for those who want to buy souvenirs or additional items during their trip. It also allows for more organized packing, where different compartments can be designated for specific items of clothing or items, making it easier to access and repack during the journey.

Manageability and resilience are other essential factors to consider. It is best to test how well the wheels ride over different surfaces before you buy them. The piece of luggage that proves its worth on airport tiles and cobblestone streets will prove indispensable when traveling internationally. Four-wheeled "spinner" cases are generally easier to move over flat surfaces; they require less effort than two-wheeled alternatives as they are pushed rather than pulled. However, their practicality diminishes on uneven surfaces, so a bag with two wheels may prove more reliable (Tips for Choosing the Best Travel Bag, n.d.).

Durability is not just limited to wheels and handles. The quality of the zippers, the robustness of the fabric or the materials used, and the seams must all withstand the rigors of the journey. Cheap luggage saves money but can cause considerable inconvenience if it breaks during the journey. You can rest assured if you choose well-rated brands known for their reliability. While high-end brands are often associated with high prices, there are also affordable options that offer excellent resilience without being too expensive. Good luggage should survive several trips before it shows the first signs of wear.

When choosing your baggage, you should always consider many airlines' strict hand baggage restrictions, especially low-cost airlines. The standard hand luggage dimensions in Europe may not correspond to the regulations of American airlines, which often require smaller dimensions. You can avoid last-minute hassles and unexpected baggage fees by finding out these details in advance. Weight restrictions can also vary, so choosing a lightweight yet sturdy bag can make a big difference in meeting these guidelines.

Different types of luggage meet different needs. A soft backpack is perhaps the most practical option for short trips. It fits easily into luggage compartments and offers the option of having both hands free, which is an advantage in busy train stations or marketplaces. Backpacks with internal frames are similar but offer more support and are ideal for rougher travel conditions where you may be hiking or walking long distances. Rolling bags, whether as hand luggage or in a larger version, are practical at airports and hotels but can become unwieldy on uneven terrain.

79

If you prefer versatility, you can opt for a wheeled rucksack, which combines easy transportation on wheels with the option of carrying the rucksack on your back. However, these hybrid models often weigh more due to the wheels and retractable handle, which often limits the amount of items you can pack. Weighing up these characteristics ensures that the selected piece of luggage meets the specific requirements of the trip.

The color and appearance of the luggage also influence its practicality. Darker colors show less soiling and wear over time, so they still look good even after many trips. However, colorful bags stand out on the baggage carousels and make it easier to find your belongings quickly in crowded baggage claim areas. Personal preferences are decisive in this decision, but functionality should always outweigh aesthetics.

One aspect often overlooked is the availability of guarantees or warranties offered by the manufacturer. Luggage that comes with a guarantee shows that the brand is trustworthy and focuses on quality. Such products are built to last and offer peace of mind that any defects or problems will be rectified, improving the longevity of the investment.

Consideration of Baggage Restrictions

Adhering to weight restrictions when packing is crucial to avoid unforeseen charges and problems. Airlines, especially low-cost airlines, often have strict regulations regarding the permitted weight of hand and checked baggage. These restrictions vary from airline to airline and can also differ depending on the ticket class and destination.

Before you start packing, you should find out about the weight restrictions of the respective airline. In Europe, many airlines, such as Ryanair and EasyJet, only allow 10 to 24 pounds for hand baggage, while the permitted weight for checked baggage varies between 30 and 46 pounds depending on the fare. In the USA, hand baggage restrictions are often more generous, but check-in fees can be high if you exceed the weight limit. Knowing these details in advance allows you to adapt your packing strategy accordingly and avoid excess baggage charges. As a rule, the permitted packing dimensions and weight restrictions are specified when booking flight tickets.

A digital luggage scale is a practical aid for complying with weight restrictions. With such a scale, you can weigh your luggage at home and ensure you do not exceed the permitted weight. This can be particularly helpful if you want souvenirs or additional items during your trip. Another way to save weight is to stow heavy items in your hand luggage as long as they comply with safety regulations.

For longer trips, where you may need more items and clothing, you can reduce the weight by cleverly repacking and using compression bags. We will go into this in more detail in a moment. Compression bags not only help to minimize the volume of bulky items but also help you distribute the weight more evenly to avoid excessive weight in your luggage. In many cases, it is advisable to carry some heavier items with you on your journey, such as a jacket or sturdy shoes, to reduce the weight in your suitcase.

The contents of your hand baggage should also be packed carefully so as not to exceed the permitted weight. Airlines often check the weight of hand baggage, and if it is over the limit, additional charges may apply. Ensure your hand luggage complies with the prescribed dimensions and weight to avoid stress at the airport.

81

Space-Saving Packing Techniques

Optimizing the space in your luggage while reducing the contents is essential for stress-free travel. Efficient packing ensures that everything you need fits in your suitcase and makes it easier to find specific items during your trip. Here are some practical tips to help you achieve this goal.

One of the simplest and most effective techniques for saving space is to roll up your clothes instead of folding them. If you roll your clothes up tightly, you can significantly reduce the space they take up and fit more in your luggage. This method not only saves space but also helps to reduce wrinkles. For example, T-shirts and jeans can be rolled up without overly creasing. In contrast, shirts and formal wear must still be folded carefully to keep their shape. Nevertheless, the rolling technique works wonders for most casual garments. This is practical for long journeys where space is at a premium.

Bulky items such as sweaters and jackets are often the main reason they take up too much space in your luggage. This is where compression bags come into play. Compression bags work by displacing air from the inside, compressing bulky clothing items to a fraction of their original size. These bags free up valuable space and ensure that your belongings are stored neatly. Many travelers swear by compression bags to pack seasonal clothing such as winter coats and thick sweaters, which are necessary but take up much space. Compressing these clothing items creates enough space for other essential items and reduces the risk of overpacking.

Another essential tool for efficient packing is the use of packing cubes. Packing cubes help you categorize your things so that you can organize them and find them more quickly on your trip. For example, you can use one cube for tops, another for bottoms and another for other items or underwear. Thanks to the structured organization offered by the packing cubes, you can stack them neatly in your suitcase and make the most of every inch of available space. In addition to easy handling, packing cubes often offer other advantages, such as compression zippers, which further reduce the volume of your packed items. The use of packing cubes maximizes space and ensures a transparent system in the suitcase, which avoids chaos when unpacking at the destination.

Hygiene articles may be small but can become unwieldy if not packed efficiently. Leak-proof containers are a decisive factor in this respect. These containers prevent spills and other items in your luggage from being affected. They are also designed to save space. Instead of taking large bottles of shampoo, conditioner or lotion with you, pour these liquids into smaller, travel-sized containers. This saves space and complies with the liquid regulations for hand luggage. Another tip is to opt for solid hygiene products such as bar shampoos and soaps, which take up less space and weigh less than their liquid counterparts.

By combining these strategies - rolling clothes, using compression bags, packing cubes and leak-proof containers - you can significantly improve the space available in your luggage while keeping everything well organized and easily accessible. This ensures a smooth packing experience and a stress-free journey.

Sustainable Packing and Environmentally Friendly Travel Products

Reducing environmental impact through sustainable packaging practices is essential for responsible travel. Choosing what you carry and how you pack it can significantly reduce your

83

environmental footprint as you enjoy your adventures. Consider practical strategies to help you pack sustainably and travel safely.

Using environmentally friendly luggage made from recycled or sustainable materials is an essential first step. Many companies now offer suitcases and bags made from used plastic, organic cotton or other renewable resources. For example, brands such as Patagonia and Samsonite offer eco-friendly product ranges that ensure your luggage is ethically produced. These alternatives are often more durable and made to withstand different travel conditions, which means they will need to be replaced less often and will generate less waste. Buying sustainable luggage pays off because it promotes longevity and reduces environmental impact.

Taking reusable items with you is another effective way to avoid single-use plastic when traveling. A high-quality, BPA-free water bottle is essential. Brands like Nomader offer water bottles that fold up for easy storage, so you never have to repurchase bottled water when traveling (Jen, 2021). If you have versatile cutlery made of bamboo or stainless steel with you, you can avoid the plastic cutlery offered at food stalls or fast food restaurants. Combine this with a reliable shopping bag made from recycled materials, perfect for spontaneous trips or souvenir shopping. These items fulfill their purpose and promote mindful consumption, making sustainability even more integrated into everyday life.

If you opt for solid hygiene products and biodegradable products, you can also significantly reduce waste and the burden of carrying heavy liquid packaging. Conventional liquid shampoos, conditioners and lotions are mainly water and are supplied in non-recyclable plastic packaging. Solid alternatives such as shampoo bars, conditioners and creams make plastic containers superfluous and generally last longer. Companies such as Ethique produce solid bars free from chemicals and require little packaging (Packing

Light - Eco Life Zone, 2023). These compact, lightweight products also ensure you comply with airline regulations for liquids in hand luggage. Biodegradable items such as bamboo toothbrushes and tablets offer environmentally friendly alternatives to conventional personal care products.

It is essential to wear versatile pieces made from sustainable fabrics when it comes to clothing. If you choose clothes that are easily combined, you must pack fewer clothes. This ensures that each garment is suitable for multiple uses. Also, opt for organic cotton, hemp or recycled polyester, which require less water and energy than conventional fabrics. Brands such as prAna and Eileen Fisher offer stylish travel clothing made from sustainable materials. These garments can be combined to provide warmth, dress you up for formal occasions or be worn casually so you can adapt to different situations without lugging around extra clothes. With timeless garments that complement each other, you will always be equipped for different occasions and not have to pack too much - a win-win situation for you and the environment.

Adaptation to Local Dress Code and Cultural Expectations

Traveling to different countries offers a wealth of experiences but also requires respect and sensitivity to local customs, especially regarding dress codes. Respectful and comfortable travel starts with packing clothes that fit the cultural norms of your destination. Understanding and following these principles can significantly impact your travel experience.

Before packing, you should learn about cultural norms and dress codes. In many Middle Eastern countries, such as Saudi Arabia or Kuwait, women are expected to dress modestly, meaning that shoulders, knees and hair must be covered. In Dubai, on the other hand, the dress code is more relaxed, but it is still recommended to keep your shoulders and knees covered in public. In India, especially when visiting religious sites such as the Golden Temple in Amritsar or the Taj Mahal, men and women must dress conservatively. Travelers should wear long pants and loose-fitting clothing to show respect and conform to local customs. Resources such as travel guides, blogs, and forums can provide valuable information on the appropriate attire for the country you plan to visit.

Next, you should focus on packing versatile clothes suitable for casual and formal occasions. Versatile garments such as shirts, pants and skirts in neutral colors are easy to combine depending on the occasion. In countries like Italy, where fashion is highly valued, you can dress stylishly yet respectfully. A simple blouse and trousers can be helpful for day trips to sights such as the Colosseum in Rome. You can accessorize them for a night out when you visit an elegant restaurant. This adaptability saves your luggage space and ensures you are prepared for different scenarios without needing a full closet.

Another important aspect of dressing appropriately when traveling is observing the rules of etiquette. In many cultures, modesty is a sign of respect and is strictly observed. Clothing that covers shoulders, knees and other culturally sensitive areas should be preferred. For example, if you travel to the Middle East, women should wear long dresses or an abaya that aligns with local customs. Men can also opt for long pants instead of shorts to show respect. In Thailand, especially when visiting temples such as Wat Phra Kaew in Bangkok, men and women are expected to keep their shoulders and knees covered. This shows respect for the site's religious significance and prevents unpleasant situations.

A practical tip is to use scarves or shawls to prepare for unexpected dress code requirements flexibly. Scarves are lightweight, take up little space and can quickly transform an outfit to meet modesty requirements or provide extra coverage at religious sites. They are helpful when you visit places like St. Peter's Basilica in the Vatican, where the dress code requires shoulders and knees to be covered. These accessories can also protect from the sun when traveling in hot climates, such as on a safari in Kenya or cool evenings, for example, in the Andes in Peru.

When traveling to Morocco, tourists will find that dressing modestly contributes significantly to their comfort and safety. Loose, conservative clothing can help women avoid unwanted attention and feel more comfortable around locals who may have traditional views on women's fashion. In the city of Fès, wearing a traditional djellaba can promote cultural exchange and help you integrate more seamlessly into the local community.

Even in South America, such as Peru or Bolivia, travelers often find that modest clothing allows for smoother social interaction and reduces the likelihood of standing out as an outsider. Breathable but covered clothing, such as long skirts or loose-fitting pants, can help meet the region's hot but often conservative dress standards. At the same time, they offer protection from the sun, which can be an advantage during activities such as a hike to Machu Picchu.

By combining a tank top with a cardigan or jacket, you remain versatile and are equipped for different weather conditions in the city and the countryside. In countries like Spain, you can opt for a casual outfit during the day and quickly create a more chic look in the evening by adding a jacket or blazer to a restaurant visit.

When you arrive at your destination, it is essential that you observe and adapt to local customs, as fashion standards can be very

87

different. Please pay attention to how the locals dress and try to imitate their style. While this does not mean you must ditch your style, slightly adapting your wardrobe, such as wearing traditional patterns in Southeast Asia or simple, elegant outfits in France, can promote a positive cultural exchange and show respect for the community you visit.

Dressing respectfully not only helps you fit in but also demonstrates cultural sensitivity and encourages positive interactions with locals. In Japan, for example, where cleanliness and style are essential, more formal, neat clothing shows that you value the cultural norms. If the locals see that you are respecting their customs and traditions, they are often friendlier and more open to talking to you. This mutual respect enhances the travel experience and makes it even more enriching and memorable.

Well-planned clothing aligns with the general goal of traveling efficiently and without stress. This also minimizes the likelihood of you getting into awkward or embarrassing situations regarding your clothes. This is the best way to immerse yourself in the local culture. This thoughtful approach to packing and dressing can enhance your travel experience and make it more enjoyable and respectful.

This is How Sarah Would Approach It

After planning her trip to Kyoto, booking flights and writing down the best packing strategies from Chapter 5, Sarah opted for a practical combination of a medium-sized suitcase as checked baggage and a giant backpack that she could use as hand luggage and for day trips on site. This selection enabled her to take everything she needed with her and remain flexible at the same time.

1. Choosing the Right Luggage Size

For her one-week trip to Kyoto, Sarah opted for a medium-sized suitcase (approx. 60-70 liters volume), which would be checked in as checked baggage. This site was ideal for carrying enough clothes for her planned activities, from hiking in the mountains to sightseeing and cultural events. The suitcase offered enough space to store clothes for different weather conditions and occasions without becoming too bulky or heavy. It also made it possible to take additional items, like hiking clothing and a rain jacket.

She also took a large backpack (approx. 20-30 liters) as hand luggage, which she could use for important things during the flight and later on-site for day trips. This backpack was handy for keeping electronics, snacks, and personal items, while the suitcase held most of her clothes and other items.

2. Packing Clothing and Equipment Sensibly

Sarah knew she had to take clothes for various activities, from temple visits to walks in Kyoto and hikes in the surrounding mountains. Therefore, she opted for a combination of functional, weather-appropriate clothing and a few more elegant items for evening restaurant visits.

She packed them in her checked baggage:

- **5 T-shirts**: Ideal for day trips and hikes, easy to combine.

- **3 sweaters and long-sleeved tops**: For cool evenings and temple visits.

- **2 pairs of** Weatherproof hiking trousers and intelligent trousers for evening outings.

- **1 light blazer**: To make their outfits more elegant in the evening.

- **1 rain jacket**: Weatherproof but lightweight, ideal for the changeable fall weather in Kyoto.

- **1 scarf**: Versatile, both as protection against the cold and as a covering in religious sites.

- **1 pair of hiking boots**: Robust and comfortable for the planned hikes.

- **1 pair of lightweight sneakers**: Ideal for exploring the city.

- **1 pair of smart shoes**: For evening restaurant visits.

- **Hiking accessories**: Wool socks that wick away moisture and breathable functional underwear.

She also planned the following for her hygiene items:

- **Solid shampoo and conditioner bars**: Space-saving and environmentally friendly.

- **Travel sizes for lotion, toothpaste and other hygiene products**: To save space and weight.

- **Sun cream and insect repellent**: For hikes in the countryside.

She packed the following items in her **backpack**:

- **Electronics**: Laptop, camera and chargers to stay productive during the trip and capture the experiences.

- **Snacks and an empty water bottle**: You should always be supplied with energy and hydration during your explorations.

- **A small first aid bag**: For emergencies or minor injuries on hikes.

- **Notebook and travel guide**: This is used to record spontaneous ideas or plans and to have orientation aids to hand.

Sarah weighs her suitcase with a luggage scale before departure and arrives at 31 pounds for her checked baggage. She excluded the permitted suitcase weight of only 16 pounds from the outset when booking the flight, so she booked the option for up to 46 pounds directly. In the end, she was able to maintain this value very well. She was allowed an additional 16 pounds for her hand baggage, which she also did not exceed, with a weight of 8 pounds.

3. Using Space-Saving Packing Techniques

Sarah would try out some of the key space-saving techniques from chapter four to make sure all these things fit neatly into her suitcase. She rolled up her casual clothes, such as T-shirts and pants, to save space and avoid creases. She stowed thicker clothing items, such as sweaters and jackets, in compression bags, considerably reducing the volume of these bulky items.

Using packing cubes also helped Sarah separate her clothes by category, so she always knew where to find specific clothing items. The shoes were stowed in separate bags not to soil the rest of her clothes.

4. Sustainability and Environmentally Friendly Decisions

Sarah placed great importance on sustainability when choosing her clothing and equipment. Inspired by the tips in the chapter, she opted for clothing made from sustainable materials such as organic cotton and recycled polyester. She also chose a travel bag made from recycled materials and ensured that the items she took were durable and environmentally friendly.

She also packed reusable items, such as a collapsible water bottle and bamboo cutlery, to avoid plastic during her trip. Their hygiene products, such as solid shampoos and conditioners, were also packaged sustainably and reduced their plastic consumption.

5. Respecting the Local Culture

Especially when visiting religious sites in Kyoto, Sarah knew she had to conform to the local dress code. She always had long sleeves or a scarf to cover her shoulders when visiting the temple. The tip mentioned in the chapter to take a light scarf with her proved extremely practical, as she could quickly throw it on when she entered a temple.

Sarah's carefully chosen clothes not only conformed to cultural norms but were also versatile enough to be helpful for both exploring the city and more formal occasions. Thanks to this thoughtful planning, she felt confident she would be respectfully and stylishly dressed in Kyoto.

Chapter 6: Find Affordable and Cozy Accommodation

Finding affordable and comfortable accommodation is also an essential aspect of any trip and requires careful consideration of the various accommodation options. Not all accommodations are the same, and each offers benefits and challenges that can significantly impact your budget and comfort. When looking for the perfect accommodation, travelers have to weigh up their personal preferences against practical aspects, taking cost and comfort into account.

This chapter presents different types of accommodation and assesses their advantages and disadvantages regarding affordability and comfort. From the reliable services of hotels to the unique experiences that Airbnb offers, we will look at what makes the different options attractive or less ideal for travelers. Hostels are rated for their budget-friendliness and social atmosphere. At the same time, the accommodations are highlighted for their authentic local experiences and personalized service. By the end of this chapter, you will have a comprehensive understanding of how to choose accommodation that meets your financial and comfort needs so that you can enjoy a pleasant and relaxing trip.

Comparison of Different Types of Accommodation

To find the perfect mix of affordability and comfort, knowing the advantages and disadvantages of the different types of accommodation is essential. Each accommodation type has its unique features that can affect your travel experience. Modern booking platforms such as Airbnb or Check24 also offer various filter options that allow you to quickly and precisely search for accommodation that meets your requirements. On Airbnb, for example, you can filter for accommodation with free WiFi, parking spaces or a kitchen to find the right option more quickly. On Check24, you can compare the ratings and the facilities such as pool, gym or air conditioning to ensure that your accommodation offers the desired level of comfort.

Hotel chains are often the first choice for many travelers because they are reliable and offer a comprehensive service. You can expect a certain level of consistent quality here. Most hotels provide daily housekeeping, room service, on-site restaurants, a fitness center and sometimes spas and swimming pools. These additional services make hotels attractive to those who want comfort and luxury. However, this reliability comes at a price. Hotels can be expensive, especially in central locations or peak travel times. In New York City, hotels near Times Square or Midtown Manhattan are often significantly more costly than those in the outlying districts. The higher price only sometimes justifies the effort, especially if you are planning a budget-friendly trip.

On the other hand, Airbnb offers excellent flexibility and a wide range of options for different tastes and budgets. With Airbnb, you can stay in unique accommodations such as historic houses, modern apartments or even tree houses for an exceptional experience. An example would be a stay in a traditional ryokan in Kyoto to experience the authentic Japanese way of life. In addition, many Airbnbs are equipped with kitchens and washing machines, which allows you to save money by cooking for yourself. However, this flexibility and convenience also has its disadvantages. As each accommodation is individually managed, the quality may vary. An apartment in Paris might be modern and well-equipped, while another accommodation in Berlin might not be as clean or comfortable, leading to an uneven standard of service (Harms, 2016).

Hostels are another excellent option, especially for budget-conscious travelers. They are cheaper than hotels and Airbnb and offer a great social atmosphere for backpackers and solo travelers. Hostels in cities like Amsterdam or Barcelona offer common areas where travelers worldwide can come together. These social aspects enrich the trip but can come at the expense of privacy. Most hostels offer dormitories with shared bathrooms, which does not suit everyone, especially if you are traveling as a couple or in a small group. Safety can also be an issue as you share the space with strangers (Baumgarten, 2021).

Guest houses offer a balance between the independence of Airbnb and the social aspect of hostels. These are often family-run businesses that offer a cozy environment and personal service. For example, a guest house in a village in Italy could offer authentic insights into the local culture and cuisine while you feel at home in a family atmosphere. These accommodations are generally cheaper than hotels but offer comfort and privacy. However, larger guesthouses often lack comprehensive services such as a 24-hour reception or an extensive range of facilities.

When choosing accommodation, it is essential to read reviews to make an informed decision. Platforms such as TripAdvisor, Booking.com and Airbnb allow you to view other guests' experiences. Suppose you read several positive reviews about the hotel's location in Rome, all of which mention how convenient it is to reach the Colosseum on foot. In that case, you can assume that the accommodation is strategically located. Reviewing reviews, consider recurring points such as cleanliness, service or noise level to get a balanced opinion.

Another practical tip is to use booking strategies to save money. Using comparison sites such as Check24 or Trivago, you can compare the best offers and often save money. Booking directly on the accommodation's website can also be advantageous, as many hotels offer discounts or special incentives for direct bookings. You can also access special offers or be informed about discount promotions by signing up for newsletters or loyalty programs. For example, if you are a Marriott Bonvoy member, you can receive exclusive discounts or free nights to help you cut travel costs.

Travel time also plays a vital role in pricing. If you travel in the low season or during the week, accommodation prices can often be significantly lower. For example, a trip to Venice in October offers you the opportunity to book accommodation near St. Mark's Square for a fraction of the price you would pay in the high season in summer.

By considering all of these factors and using the appropriate filter options and reviews on platforms, you can ensure that your accommodation is comfortable and affordable and perfectly complements your travel experience.

Evaluation of Reviews and Ratings

Online reviews have become indispensable for making informed decisions about accommodation when planning a trip. Busy professionals and avid travelers can greatly benefit from reading reviews to find accommodations that offer a balance between affordability and comfort. In order to use these resources effectively, it is important to know how to navigate the vast amount of information and how to interpret it.

Online platforms such as TripAdvisor, Booking.com and Airbnb collect thousands of user reviews that provide different opinions. These opinions can help potential travelers narrow down their choices based on the experiences of other users. According to a study, four out of five respondents say that TripAdvisor gives them more certainty in their booking decisions (Tripadvisor, 2019). This trust is based on the descriptive and accurate content of these reviews, which reflect the actual experiences of other travelers. For example, suppose you are looking for accommodation in Barcelona. In that case, you can find reviews of apartments in El Born or Gràcia on TripAdvisor to help you choose the right neighborhood for your trip. By reading several reviews, you can make sure you have a clear picture of what to expect.

Filtering online reviews according to personal preferences is a practical strategy for making the most of them. Rating platforms often offer various filters, such as family-friendly, inexpensive, luxurious or for solo travelers, which can help you quickly find the most critical information. By focusing on reviews that match your specific needs and interests, you can save time and narrow down the overwhelming flood of information. Let us say you are looking for quiet accommodation in Venice. In this case, you could filter for reviews focusing on secluded areas or quiet boutique hotels in neighborhoods like Cannaregio to find the right setting for your trip.

Social media and forums are also rich sources of real-life experiences and insights. On platforms such as Facebook groups, Reddit and specialized travel forums, travelers can share detailed reports about their stays, often highlighting aspects not included in traditional reviews. These areas can help find up-to-date information and niche recommendations. The exchange with a travel community can provide personal advice and insider tips that are less easy to find on the usual review portals. For example, suppose you are unsure which areas of London are safe for women traveling alone. In that case, you might hear from someone on a travel forum who has recently made a similar trip and can give personal recommendations.

When using reviews, distinguishing between genuine feedback and advertising content is an important skill. Not all reviews are equal, and the reviewer's credibility plays a vital role in the reliability of the information. An example would be if you are looking for accommodation on Airbnb and notice that the host's reviews are almost exclusively positive and very short - this could indicate fake reviews. Look for detailed, balanced reviews that mention both positive and negative aspects. An example of this would be a review in which a guest praises the central location of an apartment in Paris but also points out that the noise from the street could be disturbing at night.

Another way to ensure accuracy is to consider the timeliness of the ratings. Respondents say that the latest content is most important to travelers. 78% focus on the latest reviews (Tripadvisor, 2019). The more recent the rating is, the more likely it is to reflect the property's current condition, including recent renovations, management changes or newly added amenities. For example, if you want to book a hotel in Berlin, more recent reviews can tell you whether the recently announced renovation has been completed.

When looking at reviews, look for consistent themes mentioned in several reviews. Suppose several guests point out poor service, problems with cleanliness or noisy surroundings. In this case, these are warning signals that should not be ignored. Conversely, recurring mentions of positive features such as friendly staff, excellent location or comfortable beds can increase the attractiveness of an accommodation. For example, if several reviews for a hotel in Tokyo repeatedly mention the excellent access to the Yamanote Line, you can be confident that the accommodation is conveniently located.

It is equally important to adopt a critical attitude when reading reviews. Sometimes, assessments can be biased or arise from atypical situations. For example, a guest with an exceptionally good or bad experience cannot represent the average stay. For example, if you are searching for a hotel in Lisbon on Booking.com, an extreme review about a one-off problem with room service might not reflect the overall experience. It is advisable to read several reviews to get a balanced picture.

Finally, it would be best to look at the validity of photos posted by previous guests. Unlike professional marketing images, these unedited snapshots accurately reflect the current state of the accommodation. They can reveal details that may not be mentioned in text reviews, such as the room size, the condition of the bathroom and the quality of the view. Photos showing accommodation in Athens, for example, could help you see the actual view of the Acropolis before you book.

By making targeted use of online reviews, you can ensure that your accommodation meets expectations and that your trip is as pleasant as possible.

Location of the Accommodation

The choice of location of your accommodation is a decisive factor that influences both the comfort and the cost of your trip. Depending on the type of trip and the planned activities, it may be advantageous to choose either central accommodation or accommodation on the city's outskirts or in the surrounding area. Each option has advantages and disadvantages, which you should consider when deciding.

Accommodation in the city center offers numerous advantages. On the one hand, you are usually near the main sights, restaurants and shopping facilities. This saves time and transportation costs and allows you to be more spontaneous as you can easily reach many places on foot. If you plan a trip to Rome, for example, central accommodation near the Pantheon or the Colosseum could allow you to explore these sights without traveling long distances. The most significant advantage of a central location is convenience. You can quickly return to your accommodation between explorations to take a break or freshen up before enjoying the evening. This proximity to the most important places is invaluable, especially for city breaks or business trips.

However, central accommodation also has its disadvantages. The costs in city centers are often significantly higher than in the immediate vicinity outside the city center. In addition, these areas, especially in tourist hotspots, can be crowded and noisy, offering less peace. Especially in popular destinations such as New York or London, accommodation in the city center often comes at a higher price, which can be a challenge for travelers on a limited budget.

Accommodation outside the city center often offers a cheaper alternative. Travelers on a tight budget can save money by choosing a hotel or vacation apartment on the city's outskirts without being too far from the center. An example of this would be Paris, where accommodation in districts such as La Défense or Saint-Denis is significantly cheaper than in the city center but still offers good connections to the city center. The most significant advantage of accommodation on the city's outskirts is the lower costs, not only for accommodation but often also for restaurants and shopping facilities. In addition, these areas often offer more peace and space, making them ideal for travelers who prefer a more relaxed atmosphere.

However, there are disadvantages here, too. Accommodation outside the city center usually requires good transport connections to get to the sights quickly. This can be an ideal compromise in cities like London, where the subway provides a fast and regular connection between the suburbs and the center. However, it is essential to ensure that travel times and costs remain manageable; otherwise, the savings in accommodation costs will be offset by higher transportation costs. Another disadvantage is the reduced flexibility. For example, if you want to attend a show downtown in New York, staying in a suburb like Queens or Brooklyn could mean longer travel times, incredibly late at night when public transportation is less frequent.

A compromise could be to choose accommodation outside the city center but close to good transport links. Cities like Berlin, Munich, or Tokyo offer extensive and reliable subway or train networks that allow you to reach the sights easily while benefiting from cheaper accommodation costs. An example would be choosing accommodation in Shibuya or Ueno in Tokyo instead of the more expensive Shinjuku district. These areas offer excellent transport connections so you can get to the city center quickly but benefit from cheaper accommodation costs.

Therefore, the choice of location for your accommodation depends on your travel preferences, your budget and the activities you have planned. While central accommodation offers the advantage of being close to the sights, locations in the surrounding area can be more affordable and quieter. A well-connected suburb could be the ideal solution to save costs without sacrificing convenience and flexibility.

101

Booking Strategies to Save Money

Developing strategies that help you secure low prices is essential to optimize your travel budget effectively. One of the most effective tactics is to book during periods of low demand. Travel prices vary considerably depending on the season, day of the week and even time of day. During the high season - such as public holidays, weekends or summer vacations - accommodation prices often rise sharply due to high demand. In contrast, you can save considerably in the low season or during the week. For example, If you plan a trip to Venice in late spring or early fall, you can benefit from lower accommodation costs and enjoy the more pleasant weather while the tourist crowds stay away.

Another clever method is to combine accommodation with other travel services. Many travel portals such as Expedia, Travelocity or Check24 offer package deals where you can book flights, hotels and rental cars together. These packages are often cheaper than if you book the services individually. Let us say you are planning a trip to Lisbon and find a package on Expedia that offers you a 20% discount if you book your flight and hotel together. This approach not only saves money but also simplifies the booking process. In addition, many credit card companies offer special deals where you earn reward points or cashback when you book through specific partner sites, allowing you to make further savings.

Flexibility in travel dates and locations can also make a big difference. Postponing travel dates by just a few days can result in considerable savings. With tools such as Google Flights or Skyscanner, you can use flexible date options to find the cheapest days for your trip. For example, you could fly on a Thursday instead of a Friday and reduce the price of your flight by up to €100. If you are also open to alternative destinations, you could find hidden gems that are both affordable and culturally enriching. Instead of visiting the expensive cities of Paris or Rome, you could travel to Porto or Bologna, which offer an equally rich cultural offering but are far more affordable.

Another valuable tip is to sign up for notifications and newsletters to be informed about price reductions and special offers. Travel portals and airlines often offer last-minute deals or flash offers sent via email or apps like Scott's Cheap Flights. These platforms regularly notify you of heavily discounted flights from your preferred departure airport. For example, you can set up notifications for flights to Thailand and strike immediately if the price is reduced. Following travel companies on social media is also helpful, as many exclusive discounts or competitions are only published on these platforms.

Lesser-known tips for booking accommodation include negotiating prices for more extended stays. Many landlords on platforms such as Airbnb or Booking.com offer discounts if you book accommodation for a week or longer. For example, in Barcelona, you can get a discount of 10-20% on the total price of a seven-day stay. Another trick is to book non-cancellable fares, often cheaper if you are sure your travel plans are set.

Early morning can also be a good time for bookings. Travel portals like Booking.com often update their prices in the early morning hours, and you might find a better deal before demand picks up again later in the day.

Traveling can be expensive, but with proper planning and innovative strategies, you can find comfortable accommodation that will not break your budget. If you incorporate these tips into your travel planning - from booking in the low season to taking advantage of package deals and being flexible with your travel dates - you can save considerably without compromising quality

103

and comfort. Over time, finding bargains will become a natural part of your travel preparation, and you will find that it is possible to enjoy quality stays while optimizing your travel budget.

Find Unique and Sustainable Accommodation

Travelers have several attractive options when choosing accommodation that combines uniqueness and environmental awareness. Boutique hotels, eco-friendly lodges, certified green hotels and local host families offer a variety of experiences that can make for an unforgettable and sustainable trip.

Boutique hotels are ideal for anyone looking for personal service and unique design. In contrast to large hotels, boutique hotels are often characterized by unique architecture and furnishings that reflect the local culture. For example, the Hotel Estalagem da Ponta do Sol on Madeira is a boutique hotel on a cliff offering breathtaking views of the Atlantic Ocean. The hotel combines minimalist architecture with traditional Portuguese elements. Personalized service is a hallmark of boutique hotels; staff often go out of their way to make each guest's stay memorable. Tailor-made experiences such as private city tours or exclusive wine tastings are often included. In Florence, many boutique hotels in historic buildings, such as the Hotel Brunelleschi, offer unique insights into the city's culture and history. These establishments often offer fewer rooms, which makes for a more exclusive and intimate atmosphere, ideal for travelers looking for a quiet and relaxed environment.

Eco-friendly lodges are a growing trend in sustainable travel. These lodges have been designed to have minimal environmental impact by using recycled materials and renewable energy. An excellent example is the Lapa Rios Lodge in Costa Rica, which uses solar panels and a water recycling system to minimize its ecological footprint. The lodge offers guided tours where guests can experience the local wildlife and allows travelers to participate in conservation projects such as planting trees or protecting endangered species. Longitude 131° Lodge in Australia is also an eco-friendly accommodation that is integrated into the landscape of Uluru-Kata Tjuta National Park and offers its guests environmentally friendly experiences, such as astronomical tours and sustainable local cuisine.

For travelers who want to actively participate in sustainable projects, lodges offer guests the opportunity to work in local communities. At the Sabyinyo Silverback Lodge in Rwanda, for example, guests can take part in programs to protect mountain gorillas and support the local community by creating jobs and promoting educational programs.

Certifications play a crucial role in identifying high sustainability standards in green hotels. Organizations such as LEED (Leadership in Energy and Environmental Design) and EarthCheck offer certifications confirming guests that their accommodation is environmentally friendly. For example, the Puri Dajuma Eco-Resort in Bali was awarded an EarthCheck certificate for using sustainable wastewater treatment and solar energy. Travelers should look for such certifications when booking to ensure that the accommodation implements sustainable practices. The Green Key certificate is Less well-known but crucial; it often meets stricter standards than conventional green hotels. A practical tip: Platforms like Booking.com or Expedia offer filter options for environmentally friendly accommodations that use these certifications. So you can search specifically for sustainable hotels.

Another example of sustainable accommodation is the Hoshinoya Resort in Japan, which combines traditional Japanese architecture

105

with environmentally friendly technology, including geothermal energy and heat recovery systems. Such accommodation offers comfort and innovative solutions to protect the environment.

For travelers looking for an immersive cultural experience, homestays or local tourism programs offer a unique way to immerse yourself in the culture while traveling sustainably. These options allow travelers to stay with local families and participate in daily activities. For example, the G Adventures Local Living program offers the opportunity to live with an Italian family in Tuscany, participate in wine tastings and cook traditional dishes. In Nepal, there are programs where travelers can live in small mountain villages and work on agricultural projects. These programs promote cultural exchange and help communities strengthen their local economies and preserve their cultural heritage.

Careful selection of accommodation allows comfort, sustainability and cultural engagement to be combined. Boutique hotels offer unique experiences with local charm, while eco-friendly lodges focus on sustainability and conservation. Certifications such as LEED and EarthCheck offer the certainty that the hotel implements green practices. Host families and local tourism programs allow you to gain deep cultural insights and promote mutual respect and understanding for the communities you visit. A lesser-known tip: Many host families also offer short-term stays so that you can experience different cultures during a single trip. By choosing such accommodation, you support the local economy, reduce your ecological footprint, and contribute to a more sustainable and enriching journey.

More Security When Choosing Accommodation

When choosing accommodation for a trip, safety is the top priority. Ensuring a safe stay can significantly improve the overall experience of a trip and reduce the stress of planning. Here are some practical tips to keep your accommodation safe:

One of the first steps to prioritize safety is to check reviews that explicitly focus on safety aspects and feedback from solo travelers. Platforms such as TripAdvisor, Booking.com and Airbnb offer valuable insights into previous guests' experiences. For example, if you are looking for accommodation in Istanbul, you can filter specifically for reports from women traveling alone or LGBTQ+ travelers to make sure the accommodation is safe. Testimonials can point to security features such as well-lit entrances, video surveillance or digital locks. You can also search Airbnb specifically for accommodations that are Superhosts, as these often meet higher standards in terms of safety and service. Search terms such as "women-friendly" or "safe for solo travelers" can also help you find suitable accommodation (Queer Adventurers, 2023).

The choice of accommodation location plays a decisive role. It is important to choose accommodation in well-lit and populated areas. Well-lit streets deter criminal activity and provide additional safety, especially when returning at night. In a city like Berlin, you could choose accommodation in the Prenzlauer Berg district, known for its safety and good public transport connections. Use Google Street View to get an impression of the area in advance. If you see many cafés, stores and lively squares nearby, you can be sure that the area is lively and safe.

The security of the accommodation itself is just as important. Ensure the hotel or vacation apartment has robust locks on the doors and windows and 24-hour reception or security staff. Many

107

Airbnb landlords now offer digital door locks, which provide additional security as you do not have to worry about lost keys. If you are staying in cities like New York or Barcelona, choose accommodation that offers video surveillance and emergency procedures. One way to feel safe is to ask the hotel staff for the best emergency exits or look at a map of the building with the emergency exits to be prepared. Some hotels also have unique security apps that make calling for assistance at the touch of a button possible.

Technology can also help you improve your safety. Apps like GeoSure give you a real-time safety rating for specific neighborhoods. This app rates areas in categories such as physical safety, health risks or LGBTQ+ acceptance and provides valuable information on how to avoid unsafe areas. You can also use travel apps such as SafeTrek to contact the local authorities immediately in an emergency.

For women and LGBTQ+ travelers, looking for inclusive and safe accommodation is particularly important. Many boutique hotels and guesthouses label themselves as women-friendly or LGBTQ+-friendly. One example is the Axel Hotel in Madrid, which has established itself as an LGBTQ+-friendly accommodation and takes special safety precautions to meet the needs of its guests. Such accommodations often offer trained staff and safety policies designed to prevent harassment or discrimination, creating a safe environment for all travelers (Queer Adventurers, 2023).

Before you make a final decision, you can take additional precautions. It can be helpful to specify a second guest when booking, even if you are traveling alone, to give the impression that you are not alone. You should also ensure that friends or family know your itinerary and check on you regularly. A helpful tip is to choose a room on an upper floor, as these are more difficult to access and offer you more privacy. A room with a view of an inner courtyard or a less busy street can also be safer and quieter.

Safety in the room should also be taken into account. Bringing personal locks for bags or valuables is an easy way to secure your belongings. It would be best to use the "Do not disturb" sign to prevent anyone from entering your room for no reason. A door stopper or an additional portable door lock can provide additional protection, especially in Airbnb accommodation or older hotels where several keys may be in circulation. If you are carrying sensitive electronic devices, a USB data blocker can be helpful to prevent devices from being hacked when charging at public charging stations.

Paying attention to your surroundings is essential when you are out and about. A friendly relationship with the hotel staff can also be an advantage. The staff often have a good overview of security in the area and can give you tips on which areas you should pay particular attention to. For example, hotel staff can recommend ways to get around the city safely in cities such as Bangkok or Mexico City. Apps such as CityMapper also provide information on safe pedestrian and public transport routes. When you leave the hotel, you should always appear confident and act as if you know your way around - this often deters potential threats. If you pretend to be meeting someone or going to a planned meeting, this gives the impression that you are not traveling alone.

Finally, it is advisable to know the exact address of your accommodation, especially if you are using cabs or carpooling. Before setting off, you should always check the vehicle's license to ensure it is a reputable service and ask the driver to drop you off directly at your accommodation. This prevents misunderstandings and ensures a safe arrival.

109

By using technological tools such as safety apps, checking reviews and considering safety precautions when choosing accommodation, you can make your trip safer and less stressful.

This is How Sarah Would Approach It

Once Sarah had organized the flights and transport for her trip to Kyoto, she turned her attention to finding suitable accommodation. She wanted a mix of comfort, affordability and an excellent location to make her exploration of the city and the surrounding area as pleasant as possible. With the help of the strategies described in Chapter 6 and the use of rating platforms, she compiled a shortlist of possible accommodations and finally made a well-considered choice.

1. Choosing the Right Type of Accommodation

Sarah began by researching the different types of accommodation that would suit her needs. As she wanted to spend a week in Kyoto and explore both the city's cultural sights and the surrounding natural areas, she was looking for comfortable and affordable accommodation.

Initially, she thought of hotels that offer high service and comfort. She found some well-rated hotels in Kyoto that offered her a central location. However, the high-season prices were high, and Sarah wondered whether she would overspend her budget this way. As she was also looking for a more authentic experience, she wondered whether a different accommodation would be more suitable.

Airbnb was another option that offered her greater flexibility. Sarah came across several exciting offers, including a traditional ryokan where she could experience Japanese hospitality first-hand. This option was very tempting as it allowed her to experience the country's culture uniquely. Some of the Airbnb she considered also offered practical amenities such as a kitchen, which allowed her to cook for herself occasionally and save money on restaurant visits.

Guest houses were an exciting alternative, as they offered a cozy, familiar atmosphere. She found several charming guesthouses that offered a good balance between comfort and authenticity, and these accommodations were also slightly cheaper than hotels.

2. Creating a Shortlist and Viewing Ratings

Once Sarah had decided on the types of accommodation that suited her needs, she put together a shortlist of her top options:

1. **Hotel Granvia Kyoto**: This centrally located hotel with good reviews is right next to the main train station. It offers excellent service, a gym and various restaurants but is more expensive than the other options.

2. **Airbnb—Traditional Ryokan: This cozy ryokan with tatami mats and futons** promises an authentic Japanese experience. It was slightly cheaper than the hotel and had a great location near the Gion district.

3. **Guest house Ohanabo**: A charming, family-run house representing a good compromise between comfort and price. It offered simple but clean rooms and a hearty Japanese breakfast that was consistently praised in the reviews.

Sarah read the reviews on TripAdvisor, Booking.com and Airbnb to make the best choice. She paid particular attention to recurring comments on cleanliness, service and the location of the

111

accommodation. Hotel Granvia Kyoto was repeatedly praised for its central location and excellent service, while the ryokan was highlighted on Airbnb for its authenticity and hospitality. The Ohanabo guest house received much praise for its family atmosphere and proximity to the main sights.

3. Weighing Up Location and Affordability

As Sarah planned to spend much time in the old town of Kyoto and the Gion district, the location of the accommodation was a decisive factor. The Hotel Granvia offered an unbeatable central location right next to the train station, which was convenient for the planned day trips to the surrounding area. However, Sarah wondered whether she was prepared to pay the higher price for this convenience.

The ryokan on Airbnb was also conveniently located near the Gion district, which she was keen to explore. It also offered the advantage that she could experience traditional Japanese life first-hand and was slightly cheaper than the hotel.

Although the Ohanabo guest house was a little outside the city center, it was well connected by public transport. It was the cheapest option on their list, and its proximity to the sights made it attractive.

4. Applying Booking Strategies and Final Decision

After weighing the pros and cons, Sarah finally opted for the Airbnb Ryokan. The authentic Japanese style and the location near the Gion district won her over, and the positive reviews gave her confidence that she had made a good choice. The opportunity to spend the night in a traditional ryokan seemed like a once-in-a-lifetime experience that she did not want to miss. She also liked having a kitchen to cook for herself occasionally.

Sarah booked the ryokan through Airbnb and took advantage of the discount promotions offered by more extended stays. As she would be staying seven nights, she received a discount on the total price. She achieved a fair price even in the high season thanks to early booking and flexibility in her travel dates.

Chapter 7: Planning Activities

Planning activities is essential to maximize your time and enhance your travel experience. If you plan your vacation activities correctly, you can make the most of every moment of your trip. This reduces the stress that is often associated with traveling. If you structure your travel days well, you can visit the best sights without feeling rushed or overwhelmed. In this chapter, you will learn how to prioritize the sights to ensure that you see all the sights and still have room for spontaneous adventures. Careful planning will make your travel experiences even more fulfilling and unforgettable.

This chapter guides you through several essential aspects of activity planning. You will learn how to create a personal checklist that matches your interests through thorough research. This chapter also deals with strategies on how you can take enough time for each sight so that you can fully enjoy every moment. You will also learn about the advantages of combining the most important sights with lesser-known insider tips and how you can design your itinerary flexibly to make room for unexpected and delightful surprises. With these practical tips, both busy professionals and travel enthusiasts will find ways to optimize their travel planning and have a smooth, enriching trip.

Prioritization of the Most Important Sights

In our hectic everyday lives, planning an effective itinerary is more than just optional; making the most of our time is necessary. Concentrating on the most important sights, we can make the most of our travel experiences without feeling overwhelmed. This requires thorough research, a personal checklist of the most important sights, an appropriate time allocation for each sight and consideration of these sights when planning the entire itinerary.

Here, it also makes sense to keep a shortlist. First, select 3-4 sights you want to cover on your trip. Once you have included these, you can fill out your list with other sights that can ideally be combined with your top list.

First, it is essential to research the destinations thoroughly with the help of travel guides, blogs and tourist websites. These resources provide insightful details about crucial sights and hidden gems. For example, suppose you're planning a trip to Paris. In that case, you can get specific information about the Eiffel Tower, the Louvre or the Jardin des Tuileries, including their history and significance, in travel guides such as the Lonely Planet. In blogs, travelers share personal experiences, such as discovering an authentic side of the city when they visit the lesser-known Passages Couverts in Paris. Tourist websites provide up-to-date information on opening hours, admission prices and special events during your visit - for example, when is the best time to visit the Louvre to avoid long queues. Combining these resources will give you a comprehensive picture of each destination's offerings. This preliminary work will help you find places that match your interests and discard those that do not. This saves you valuable time and improves your travel experience.

Another critical step is the creation of checklists that are tailored to personal interests. A checklist based on individual preferences ensures a sensible and successful trip. Are you interested in history, an art lover or adventurous? Your interest determines which places you have to search for in the list. If you are interested in art, a visit to the Museum of Modern Art (MoMA) in New York or the Uffizi Gallery in Florence will be a priority. If, on the other hand, you are looking for thrills, activities such as a zip line in the Arenal Volcano National Park in Costa Rica or a climbing tour on Trolltunga in Norway should be included in your program. Creating a personal checklist will make the trip even more exciting and enjoyable

115

because each stop on your journey will be linked to your passions and curiosity.

It is just as vital that you take enough time for each sight so that you can see the most important things and don't feel rushed. Packing as many activities as possible into a single day is tempting. Nevertheless, this approach often makes you tired and less fun. Instead, you could take enough time to explore each place at your leisure. If you visit the Vatican Museum in Rome, for example, you should plan at least three hours to enjoy the Sistine Chapel and the impressive art collections instead of rushing through in just one hour. Planning breaks for photos and snacks or simply enjoying the breathtaking views rather than following a tight schedule would be advisable on a hike to the Grand Canyon.

If you plan the most important sights into your itinerary, considering the proximity and travel time between places, you can further optimize your travel plan. Well-planned routes reduce unnecessary detours and long journeys, so you can spend more time exploring instead of commuting. For example, if you are on a city trip to Barcelona, you could visit Park Güell and then the Sagrada Familia. This way you avoid long travel times and can explore both sights in one day. Tools such as Google Maps or apps like Citymapper help you to find the best routes and travel times.

Hidden insider tips, which you often find via blogs and local recommendations, give your trip an exceptional touch. Visiting the famous Acropolis in Athens is undoubtedly a must, but why not also discover the charming and lesser-known neighborhoods like Anafiotika, where you'll find small tavernas and narrow, winding alleyways that tourists often overlook? Such discoveries make your trip unique and offer an authentic insight into local life.

Proper planning involves more than just the sights you visit and how you plan your trip. An advantage is a flexible itinerary that can adapt to unexpected changes such as weather conditions or sudden closures. For example, if you are planning a boat trip to Iceland's Westfjords and the weather conditions suddenly change, you could spontaneously visit the Blue Lagoon and relax there instead. Flexibility enables spontaneous decisions that often lead to pleasant surprises.

It is also helpful to assess your strengths realistically. Too much planning can lead to exhaustion and reduce the enjoyment of the trip. Combine high-energy activities with rest periods. For example, after a strenuous hike up Table Mountain in Cape Town, you could spend a relaxing afternoon in a café on the Victoria & Alfred Waterfront. This balance ensures that your energy is maintained throughout the journey and you are not overloaded.

Avoidance of Overplanning

Avoiding overplanning is crucial in getting the most out of your trip without being exhausted or stressed. It's tempting to want to make the most of every minute and fill the day with numerous activities. But if you schedule your day too tightly, there is a risk that you won't be able to enjoy the experiences enough, and stress will build up if something doesn't go smoothly. To find a balanced daily structure, some guidelines will help you organize your day effectively without overloading yourself.

A rule of thumb for the time distribution during a travel day can be as follows: around 30 to 35 percent of your day should be planned for sleep, i.e., around 7 to 8 hours. Sufficient sleep is essential to stay physically and mentally refreshed and get the most out of your experiences every day. Especially when traveling and discovering

117

new things, your body and mind need this recovery phase to stay fit and receptive.

You should plan around 10 to 15 percent of your day, i.e., around 2 to 3 hours, for the journeys between the various locations and activities. It is advisable not to underestimate this time, as even short journeys can take longer than planned if you depend on public transport or if traffic and waiting times play a role. Waiting times can accumulate, especially in larger cities or tourist locations. Try to plan your activities in proximity to each other to distribute the distances between the stations optimally and have more time for exploration.

Just as significant as transportation are breaks, which you should consciously integrate into your daily routine. Approximately 10 to 15 percent of the day, i.e., 2 to 3 hours, should be set aside for rest periods. These breaks allow you to take a deep breath and process what you have seen. Whether you take a leisurely break in a café, stroll through small stores or linger in a quiet place, these times ensure that you can enjoy the day relaxed and balanced. Breaks also help to clear your head and maintain your energy for the rest of the day.

The remaining 40 to 50 percent of the day can then be used for activities - i.e., around 6 to 8 hours in which you can visit sights, go on excursions or discover unique places. It is essential to organize this part of the day flexibly. Although a fixed structure can help to keep an overview, there should always be room for spontaneity and unplanned discoveries. A good balance of planned and spontaneous activities is the key to a fulfilling trip. The 70/30 approach has proven beneficial: Plan about 70 percent of this time with fixed activities, but leave 30 percent of the day open for spontaneous experiences and unexpected discoveries. This will keep you flexible and prevent you from clinging too tightly to a rigid plan that could put you in a time crunch. Unless there is a single activity goal for which the entire time must be scheduled.

Planning buffer times between activities is also crucial to avoid stress. There can always be delays due to unexpectedly long distances, waiting times or because you want to stay longer at a specific location. Buffer times allow you to get from one program point to the next without haste and pressure. Instead of getting hectic if the schedule isn't met precisely, you can sit back, relax and enjoy the moment.

You should also make sure you plan no more than two or three major daily activities. Too many planned activities can quickly lead to excessive demands. Concentrating on a few intense experiences you can enjoy at leisure is better. A day spent visiting a historical site followed by an extended hike or boat trip will feel better than an overcrowded schedule with lots of short stops that you tick off and then rush to the next destination.

After all, you should be aware that spontaneity often offers the best surprises. By consciously leaving time for unexpected discoveries, you create space for unforeseen adventures. Whether you stumble upon a charming market by chance, end up in a small restaurant off the beaten track, or enjoy an unforgettable natural moment. These spontaneous experiences are often what make your trip memorable.

Book Tours and Tickets in Advance

Planning activities is essential to save time and guarantee a smooth travel experience. One of the first steps in this process is to book tours and tickets well in advance. By securing tickets for popular attractions in advance, you can ensure that you visit the sights you want and often also benefit from financial advantages such as early

119

booking discounts or package deals. Imagine arriving at a historic attraction and realizing that all the tickets are already sold out; booking in advance can avoid disappointment and make you feel prepared.

When selecting tour operators, you must choose reputable providers. Reading reviews and asking for recommendations can protect you from bad experiences. Many online platforms, including Tripadvisor and Yelp, offer customer feedback that can help assess the quality of service from different providers. For example, a family trip organized by a well-rated operator may include knowledgeable tour guides and on-time service, which enhances the overall travel experience. Trusted providers also offer better customer service, which can be invaluable if problems arise during the trip.

Flexibility in bookings must be balanced. Unexpected situations, such as sudden changes in the weather or personal emergencies, can thwart even the best-laid plans. Flexible bookings allow travelers to make last-minute changes without incurring high costs. Look out for options that offer free cancelations or rescheduling. Some airlines and hotels have relaxed their policies to accommodate these needs, especially in light of recent global events. Flexible booking strategies give you the certainty that you are flexible if your plans change.

Online resources play an essential role in modern travel planning. Websites such as Expedia, Booking.com and official tourism sites are real treasure troves of information and offers. These platforms often organize flights, accommodation, and activities in discounted packages, offering convenience and savings. They also provide user reviews, stars and detailed descriptions to help travelers make better decisions.

Expedia, for example, allows users to compare the prices of different airlines and hotels to get the best possible deal. Booking.com goes one step further by providing information on nearby attractions and transportation options, making it easier to plan the entire trip. Official tourism websites often list cultural events, local festivals and other activities that may not be widely advertised but can enrich the travel experience.

To combine all these aspects, imagine a traveler planning a week-long trip to Paris. If he books tickets for the Louvre and the Eiffel Tower months in advance, he secures admission and even receives early booking discounts. If you choose a well-rated tour operator, you can experience the city's historic sights without the usual tourist stress. Thanks to this provider's flexible policy, changes can be made quickly if the traveler decides to visit Versailles a day earlier due to the weather forecast. Using Booking.com, he finds a cozy boutique hotel in Montmartre that fits the budget and gets insights into local restaurants and hidden art galleries. The result? A carefully planned yet flexible itinerary that makes the most of every moment in Paris.

Tools and Apps for Planning Activities and Managing Itineraries

In today's fast-paced world, technology is crucial for efficient travel planning. With various apps and tools, travelers can make the most of their time and improve their overall experience without the stress generally associated with organizing trips. Choosing the right apps can significantly simplify the entire planning process by bundling all the essential information and making it accessible both online and offline.

Patrick Karban

An indispensable app is TripIt, which summarizes all your travel plans in a comprehensive itinerary. TripIt's automatic import function synchronizes your travel data directly from emails by extracting confirmations of flights, hotels, rental cars, and other bookings and organizing them into a precise itinerary. A significant advantage of TripIt is its offline availability, so you can access your booking details even without an internet connection - particularly useful in remote areas or when traveling abroad where the internet may be limited. The app also provides notifications and real-time updates if there are any changes to your itinerary, which is a huge relief when last-minute adjustments are necessary. Thanks to these functions, you save time and always have all the essential information to hand without searching through various apps or emails.

Google Travel goes one step further by providing personalized activity suggestions based on your preferences and previous travel experiences. Thanks to the integration with Google Maps, Google Travel helps you manage your flights and hotel reservations and find places of interest near your accommodation or along your route. You can see directly how long the journey times to the desired locations are and how the traffic conditions affect your plans. This helps you plan the optimal itinerary and ensures you can use every minute of your trip efficiently. If you arrive in a new city and don't know exactly where to go next, Google Travel will suggest sights, restaurants or activities you might have overlooked based on your previous interests.

For travelers who like to travel by car, Roadtrippers is an indispensable app for detailed route planning. It highlights points of interest along your route that you might not usually discover - from hidden cafés and picturesque streets to historical monuments. Practically, Roadtrippers supports collaborative planning. If you are traveling with friends or family, everyone can participate in the planning by working together on the itinerary and adding ideas. This function ensures everyone is on the same page and that the trip is optimally planned for everyone. Roadtrippers is ideal for road trips where you want to take detours off the highway to discover unique places.

Sygic Travel offers enhanced functionality with day-by-day itineraries tailored to your interests. The app has an extensive database of sights, restaurants and stores to include in your planning. The option to download maps offline is handy. This is extremely helpful in areas with poor or no internet connection, as you can easily find your way around without a constant connection. In addition, Sygic Travel offers selected travel guides that give you valuable insights into well-known sights and lesser-known places. This function is particularly suitable for travelers who want to plan their days in detail and ensure they don't miss any critical experiences.

By using these apps, you can simplify your travel planning considerably and ensure that you can react flexibly to changes and unexpected events. The combination of real-time updates, personalized recommendations and offline maps makes it possible to integrate planned and spontaneous activities into your travel day without stress. This allows you to enjoy the moment instead of worrying about organizational details.

The collaborative features of many of these apps make them particularly valuable for group travel. They promote cooperation and allow everyone on the trip to make their own contribution. This leads to a collective travel experience in which the anticipation is already shared during the planning stage, and the trip itself becomes a shared adventure.

123

Find Authentic Impressions On Site

Avoiding tourist traps is crucial for an authentic travel experience and cultural immersion. Tourist traps are often heavily advertised and attract visitors by promising a simple, albeit superficial, insight into local life. However, these places usually don't offer real experiences and can even be overpriced and disappointing. To avoid falling into these typical traps, you need to plan your trips so that you discover natural and cultural highlights.

Start with thorough research in reviews, blogs and local travel guides. Check travel forums, read Google reviews and follow local businesses or people on social media. Travel blogs written by individual travelers rather than tourism companies offer valuable insights into lesser-known places locals appreciate. For example, if you're traveling to Barcelona, a typical tourist restaurant along Las Ramblas might be overpriced and offer disappointing paella. On blogs, you might instead find recommendations for authentic places like "Can Paixano," a hidden bar near the harbor where locals drink cava and enjoy delicious bocadillos. In Rome, you can use blogs and forums to find tips on small restaurants such as "Trattoria Da Enzo" in Trastevere, which serves authentic Roman cuisine away from the crowds of tourists.

Venture beyond the typical tourist areas to experience the true essence of the destination. Using public transport instead of coaches saves money and immerses you in the locals' everyday life. For example, instead of taking an expensive tourist train in Tokyo, you can use the JR Yamanote line, which circles the entire city and offers an authentic and affordable way to explore the city. Public transportation covers areas tourists rarely venture into, offering insights into everyday life and hidden sights. If public transit is out of the question, consider ridesharing apps like Grab in Southeast

Asia or Didi in China over traditional cabs to avoid overcharging and explore places locals frequently go.

Contact with locals can significantly improve your travel experience. Talk to café staff, innkeepers and even strangers on the street to get their recommendations for the best restaurants and sights. If you are in Lisbon, for example, a conversation with a local waiter might lead him to recommend the "Mercado de Campo de Ourique" instead of the crowded "Time Out Market" hall - a less touristy but equally lively market with local delicacies. Many locals are proud of their hometowns and are happy to give insider tips that are unavailable in travel guides.

Visiting local events and festivals is another excellent way to immerse yourself in the cultural fabric of a place. For example, suppose you are traveling in Mexico City during Día de los Muertos. In that case, you might learn from a local that the Xochimilco district offers particularly authentic celebrations away from the main touristy events. Participating in such events can create unforgettable memories and provide a deep understanding of the local way of life.

Consider participating in non-profit tourism and volunteer opportunities. In Thailand, for example, you could participate in an elephant conservation project instead of booking elephant rides. These initiatives support the local population and offer unique, educational and rewarding experiences. Whether you're helping on a farm in Italy or taking part in a nature conservation project in Costa Rica, activities like these allow you to give something back and get to know your destination better at the same time.

It's better to go to smaller, family-run restaurants rather than chain restaurants to enjoy the local flair. The small restaurant "Diporto" in Athens could be a hidden insider tip. There is no menu, and you will enjoy traditional Greek dishes passed down from generation to generation. A narrow alley discovered by chance could lead to a cozy restaurant with locals that promises an authentic dining experience.

Local markets are treasure troves of culture and cuisine. At the "Mercado San Pedro" in Cusco, Peru, market vendors offer fresh, regional dishes such as "ceviche" or "anticuchos," which reflect the essence of Peruvian cuisine. Taking a culinary tour or cooking class in Chiang Mai, Thailand, can further deepen your understanding and appreciation of the local cuisine.

Sustainable travel is also closely linked to avoiding tourist traps and seeking authentic experiences. In Porto, Portugal, you can stay in a small family-run guest house instead of a large hotel and support the local economy. You also often get to know the city from a different perspective, as your hosts usually give you insider tips and personal insights.

The low season is ideal for visiting popular destinations while avoiding the overwhelming tourist crowds. In Iceland, for example, if you travel just after the peak season in the fall, you can enjoy the impressive waterfalls such as Skógafoss almost to yourself and experience the country more quietly and intensely.

This is How Sarah Would Approach It

Once Sarah had organized her accommodation and transport for her trip to Kyoto, she focused on planning her activities. She wanted to experience the main sights in the city while ensuring that her days were not overloaded. Sarah followed the tips from Chapter 7 to create a balanced and flexible itinerary that allowed for spontaneous discoveries and plenty of breaks.

1. Prioritizing the Most Important Sights

Sarah began with thorough research to make the most of her time in Kyoto. She used travel guides and blogs to find the best-known sights and hidden gems. Sarah quickly realized that some places, such as the Fushimi Inari Shrine, the Kinkaku-ji (Golden Pavilion) and the Arashiyama Bamboo Forest, should not be missed on any trip to Kyoto.

Sarah drew up a shortlist of the sights that were her top priority:

- **Fushimi Inari Shrine**: Famous for its endless torii gates, this place was a must for Sarah.

- **Kinkaku-ji (Golden Pavilion)**: The shining gold and the surrounding gardens were another highlight she didn't want to miss.

- **Arashiyama bamboo forest**: The peaceful atmosphere and the impressive bamboo forests were also at the top of her list.

- **Kyoto Imperial Palace**: She also wanted to visit this vital place to learn more about the history of Japan.

Once she had decided on these four main sights, she filled up her list with a few more attractions that were geographically close by and could easily be integrated into her daily plans:

- **Nanzen-ji Temple**: Another important temple that fitted nicely into a day when she wanted to walk along the Philosopher's Path.

- **Gion district**: When Sarah was looking for a way to experience traditional Kyoto, she planned an evening walk through the famous Gion district to experience the geisha culture.

2. Planning for Flexibility and Breaks

Sarah knew it was important not to plan too many daily activities. She, therefore, decided to block out enough time for most of the sights so that she could explore the places at her leisure. She wanted to avoid feeling stressed and, therefore, followed the rule of thumb of scheduling no more than two to three major daily activities.

One example was her day in the Arashiyama bamboo forest: Sarah planned to explore the bamboo forest in the morning and then visit the nearby Tenryu-ji temple. In the afternoon, she left herself free to spontaneously relax in one of the many small cafés by the river or, weather permitting, take a boat trip on the Hozu River.

She also planned conscious breaks for each day. For example, on the day of her visit to the Kinkaku-ji temple, she wanted to take a quiet walk through the Ryoan-ji garden in the afternoon and enjoy the meditative atmosphere of the rock garden before resting in a traditional teahouse.

3. Booking Tours and Tickets in Advance

Sarah decided to book some tours and tickets in advance to avoid long waiting times. Although the Fushimi Inari Shrine was freely accessible, she booked a guided tour for her visit to the Kyoto Imperial Palace so that she could delve deeper into the place's history. She also bought tickets in advance to visit the Kiyomizu-dera temple, as this temple is often overrun by tourists, and she was able to save time.

When booking tours, Sarah always chose providers that offered flexible cancellation policies in case her plans changed due to weather or other unforeseen events.

4. Use Apps for Activity Planning

Sarah used various apps and tools to organize her activities better. She used Google Maps to plan the routes between the sights so that she could avoid longer journeys. This helped her to structure her days efficiently without wasting too much time on transportation.

She also used the TripIt app to manage all her bookings and planned activities in one place. This allowed her to keep track of her daily plans and ensure enough time for each sight and spontaneous discovery.

5. Searching for Authentic Local Experiences

In addition to the well-known sights, Sarah was looking for authentic local experiences. In Kyoto, she was keen to attend a traditional tea ceremony performed by locals to learn more about Japanese culture. She found recommendations in travel blogs and decided on a small teahouse that was off the beaten track and was described by many visitors as particularly authentic.

She also planned an evening stroll through the Gion district, where she wanted to watch the geishas and sample local specialties in one of the small restaurants. Her research in forums and blogs had given her an insider tip for a restaurant that locals mainly frequented.

6. Avoidance of Overplanning

After all, Sarah needed to avoid overplanning. She adhered to the 70/30 rule, according to which she had about 70 percent of her time firmly planned while 30 percent was left open for spontaneous activities. This flexibility allowed her to make unexpected discoveries without a strict schedule.

129

Chapter 8: Budget Planning for Your Trip

Budgeting your trip requires careful planning and a strategic approach. This chapter is about setting and optimizing your travel budget without sacrificing quality or unforgettable experiences. If you know the principles for setting a realistic budget, you can ensure that your travel costs align with your financial means and personal preferences.

This chapter guides you through various steps to find an appropriate travel budget. It starts by assessing your financial situation and determining how much you can spend on your trip. You will learn to differentiate between fixed and variable costs, use budgeting tools to track expenses and plan financial resources for expected and unexpected costs. The chapter also offers practical tips for luxury and budget-conscious travelers so that you can enjoy an eventful trip regardless of your financial means.

Create an Accurate List of Your Expenses

Avoiding unexpected costs during a trip is the key to enjoying your vacation without financial burdens. A detailed and realistic breakdown of the essential spending categories helps to avoid unforeseen surprises and gives you more flexibility for unforgettable experiences. Determining the relevant expenditure categories is the first step towards an adequate travel budget. These categories usually include transportation, accommodation, meals, activities and miscellaneous expenses.

Transportation is one of the largest expense categories for most trips. This includes airline tickets, train tickets, rental cars, fuel, public transportation fares and other means of getting from one place to another. To calculate these costs accurately, you should research the average prices for your destination and your preferred means of transportation. For example, domestic flights are often cheaper on weekdays than on weekends. Booking flights or trains in the low season can also bring considerable savings. Those who fly during the week save around $ 90 per ticket (Average Vacation Costs in 2024, 2023).

Accommodation is also a significant expense that depends heavily on your preferences. Whether you prefer a luxury hotel, vacation apartment or hostel, each option offers different price levels. If you know the average price for overnight stays at your destination, you can make a realistic calculation. An average hotel costs around $129 per night, while Airbnb accommodation is often cheaper, especially when shared between multiple travelers (Average Vacation Costs in 2024, 2023).

Food can also make up a large part of the budget, especially if you regularly eat in restaurants. Researching local food prices and considering your eating habits to plan for these costs is helpful. On average, you can expect to pay around €58 per day for food, although you can save a lot by preparing your meals in your accommodation (Average Vacation Costs in 2024, 2023). If you only go to restaurants occasionally and use local markets or supermarkets instead, you have more financial leeway for unique culinary experiences.

Activities and entertainment are also significant expenses that can vary greatly. It would be best if you researched in advance which activities at your destination are free and chargeable. For example, hikes or visits to public parks can be free, while tickets for sights or concerts can cost between $ 7 and $ 250. Calculating these costs in advance lets you determine which activities are critical to you and which can perhaps be canceled or replaced more cheaply.

131

Various expenses such as tips, souvenirs, laundry service, and emergencies are also included in the budget. Although these costs are difficult to predict, reserving 10-15% of your total budget for unforeseen expenses is advisable. For example, if you plan a budget of § 2,000, you can set aside $ 200 to $ 300 as a buffer for unexpected costs. This keeps you flexible and equipped for all eventualities.

Tools and apps like Tripcoin, Trabee Pocket and Splitwise make managing your spending in real time more accessible. They allow you to record every transaction, categorize spending and track whether you stay within your budget. With graphical representations of your spending, you can recognize early on if you spend too much money in certain areas and take appropriate countermeasures.

You can also document your expenses in a spreadsheet to get an individual and detailed overview. This way, you can note down daily expenditures for transportation, accommodation, food and activities and compare them with your planned budget. This helps to identify trends, such as whether you are spending more money on meals than initially planned and allows you to adjust your budget continuously.

One example: If planning a seven-day trip, you could calculate the following expenses: 1,800 for transportation, $ 900 for accommodation, $ 400 for food, $ 300 for activities and $ 100 for miscellaneous expenses. With a nest egg of $ 500 for unforeseen costs, you'll have a total budget of $ 4,000. With a precise breakdown, you can better control during the trip whether you are spending too much money in certain areas or whether you can redistribute it.

Set a Realistic Travel Budget

Now that you have an accurate list of your expected expenses in different categories, the next step is to create a realistic and flexible budget that fits your financial means. Your travel budget should balance your wishes and your financial capacities. Start by reviewing your financial resources, i.e., savings, monthly income, and other sources. This way, you can ensure that your travel expenses do not hurt your ongoing obligations such as rent, loans or insurance.

Think about what kind of trip you have planned up to this point. Would you like a luxurious trip with upscale accommodation and excellent food or a budget-friendly trip with cheaper options? The answer to this question largely determines how you should prioritize your budget. Luxury travelers tend to budget more for hotels and exclusive restaurants, while budget travelers may stay in hostels and resort to street food to save money. If you know your priorities in advance, you can better assess which areas of your budget can be made more flexible.

In addition to the usual expenses for transportation, accommodation and meals, you should also consider possible fluctuations in variable costs when setting your budget. The costs can quickly add up, especially in categories such as activities or food, depending on how often you eat out or what kind of activities you choose. If you recognize which areas are particularly costly in advance, you can make adjustments before the trip.

Using budgeting tools to control your finances during the trip would be best. Apps like Mint or YNAB (You Need A Budget) allow you to track your spending in real time and adjust your budget flexibly. Mint helps you categorize your spending and receive notifications when you reach a limit. YNAB encourages you to

133

budget every dollar and consciously identify savings opportunities. With such tools, you can ensure that you don't slip into negative territory and recognize early on where you might be able to make savings.

Another important point when setting the budget is to consider unexpected events. Even the best-planned trips can require additional financial resources due to unforeseen medical expenses or delays. Therefore, always plan a nest egg of 10-15% of your budget to be prepared for such situations. This reserve gives you the security you need to avoid financial difficulties in the event of surprises.

Regularly reviewing and adjusting your budget is also essential. During the trip, the costs for certain expenses may change, or new fees may be added. If you've spent less in a category like transportation, you can reallocate that money to a particular activity or a luxurious dinner. Conversely, you can react flexibly if unexpected expenses occur in a category. This keeps you on track at all times and allows you to enjoy your trip without financial stress.

Managing Currencies and Exchange Rates

When traveling internationally, keeping fees as low as possible and exchanging currency effectively to optimize your budget is essential. If you approach these aspects strategically, you can focus more on enjoying your trip rather than fretting over financial details.

A practical way to reduce costs is to use multi-currency accounts such as Revolut or Wise. These services offer favorable exchange rates and low transaction fees in various currencies. With a multi-currency account, you can hold and spend money in several currencies without incurring the high conversion costs familiar with traditional banks. This flexibility allows you to manage your finances more efficiently when traveling and ensures you get the most out of every transaction.

Another smart move is to avoid bureaux de change at airports. These stalls often charge exorbitant fees and offer less favorable exchange rates than other offers. Instead, it would be best to consider ATMs, which usually offer better rates due to their direct connection to banking networks. Before you travel, check whether your bank charges fees for withdrawals from international ATMs and look for partners or global networks that can further minimize these costs. Here, an app such as ATM Hunter from MasterCard can also help find accessible ATMs in your area.

In addition to avoiding high fees at ATMs, it can be advantageous to take advantage of exchange rate fluctuations. With the help of apps such as XE Currency or Revolut, you can monitor exchange rates in real time and set up automatic notifications to be informed when the exchange rate is exceptionally favorable. If you keep an eye on the exchange rate, you can exchange more significant amounts in the local currency at the right time and make your budget more efficient. It also helps to bear in mind the so-called "Monday phenomenon." On Monday mornings, after the markets open, exchange rates can be temporarily less favorable before stabilizing over the week.

Another tip for saving money is to avoid dynamic currency conversions (DCC). Many ATMs and stores abroad offer you the option of paying in your home currency, which may seem convenient at first glance. However, such conversions often lead to poor exchange rates and hidden fees. It is always better to pay in

135

the local currency and leave the conversion to your bank or credit card.

Choosing a credit card without foreign transaction fees is another essential strategy to control spending abroad. Many credit card companies charge fees of between 1% and 3% on every purchase in a foreign currency. These fees can quickly add up and considerably strain your travel budget. Find out about credit cards specially developed for international travel and do not charge these fees. With these cards, you can shop flexibly worldwide without incurring additional costs.

If you want to use your smartphone for banking apps or monitoring exchange rates while traveling, it makes sense to use an eSIM card if your device supports this feature. eSIM cards offer the advantage of instant access to mobile internet without having to change a physical SIM card. They are flexible and often cheaper than international roaming charges. You can activate local data plans in different countries and always have access to mobile services essential for managing your finances. This is particularly useful if you want to receive real-time notifications about exchange rate changes or spending limits when you're out and about.

For emergencies, carrying a reserve of cash in common currencies such as US dollars or euros is always advisable. Although digital payments are becoming increasingly important, there are still places in some countries and regions that only accept cash. In addition, unexpected scenarios can occur, such as non-functioning ATMs or technical faults. In such cases, it is reassuring to know that you have a small amount of cash with you to be able to react to such situations at short notice.

An often-overlooked tip is looking out for cashback portals that offer discounts for international purchases. Many credit cards offer additional cashback bonuses or discounts for certain foreign transactions. You can benefit from extra savings when booking hotels, flights or restaurants abroad.

It is also worth actively negotiating in countries that prefer cash payments. Especially in parts of Asia or South America, it is possible to pay with cash and receive discounts, as sellers avoid credit card fees in this way. This can be particularly helpful for larger purchases or tours.

Another valuable tip is that international travelers can benefit from tax refunds in many countries. Particularly in the EU and Asia, visitors can reclaim VAT on purchases over a certain amount. To do this, you must submit the relevant application at the time of purchase and complete the process when you leave. This can mean considerable savings on high-priced items such as electronics or clothing.

Find Free and Inexpensive Activities

One of the most exciting aspects of planning a trip is discovering budget-friendly activities that will enhance your travel experience without burdening you with high costs. Whether you're a busy professional looking to make the most of your travel experiences or a travel enthusiast looking for practical tips, these strategies can help you get more for less.

When planning a trip, free attractions should be on your list. Many cities worldwide offer days for museums and cultural sites to waive admission fees. For example, many museums in London, such as the British Museum or the Tate Modern, have permanent free admission. In other cities, such as Paris or Rome, there is often a "Museum Sunday" on which entrance fees to many cultural sites

137

are waived. These opportunities offer you the perfect chance to immerse yourself in the local culture without spending a penny. Parks and street markets also provide great experiences that are free of charge. Public parks are not only places for recreation but often also venues for free concerts, performances or other events. In cities like New York, Central Park is a prime example that regularly hosts free events such as theater performances or live music. A walk through the park also allows you to observe the daily routine of the locals and soak up the city's atmosphere.

Adventures in nature are another great way to enjoy the natural beauty of your destination. Activities such as hiking, cycling, or simply picnicking connect you with the surroundings and offer a healthy and inexpensive leisure activity. In many national parks worldwide, such as Yosemite National Park in the USA or the Alps in Europe, you can explore breathtaking landscapes without incurring significant costs. There are also many opportunities in urban regions: In cities like Lisbon, for example, you can enjoy spectacular panoramas of the city for free from the miradouros (viewpoints). A picnic with local specialties in a picturesque location lets you experience the country's culture and cuisine relaxedly. Such excursions into nature, such as a bike tour through the Little Big Econ State Forest in Orlando, not only offer peace but also direct contact with the animal and plant world and enrich your trip with authentic experiences (BUDGET-FRIENDLY ORLANDO ACTIVITIES, 2021).

Using online resources and local information can uncover secret highlights that are both fun and inexpensive. Websites, travel blogs and social media platforms often list accessible or affordable activities for various destinations. Another helpful source is apps such as Spotted by Locals or LikeALocal, which give you recommendations from locals and thus allow you to discover places that tourists often overlook. In Berlin, for example, you can stumble upon hidden backyards adorned with street art or discover small, cozy cafés in Paris that are not listed in the typical travel guides. Contact with locals in forums or community groups, such as Reddit or Facebook, can also give you valuable insider tips. Especially in smaller towns or more remote regions, locals often know where to find the most beautiful views or the quietest parks. This way, you can intensify your travel experience without spending much money.

If you want to save money, you should opt for self-guided tours or self-planned excursions. Many destinations offer free or inexpensive audio guides or city tour apps that give you detailed information on the most important sights and allow you to create your tour. In cities such as Barcelona or Rome, you can stroll through the old town, discover impressive architecture, and at the same time determine your journey. This method saves you money and gives you the flexibility to stay longer in the places that particularly fascinate you. Free brewery tours, such as those at the Orlando Brewing Company, also offer a unique opportunity to experience local cultures and traditions without digging deep into your pockets (BUDGET-FRIENDLY ORLANDO ACTIVITIES, 2021).

For those who prefer a structured approach, planning is crucial. Do your research before you leave and create a preliminary itinerary with free and inexpensive activities. You can also use apps like Meetup to participate in free or low-cost events and group activities organized by locals. There are often hiking groups, yoga in the park or city tours offered by locals for a small donation or even free of charge. These platforms provide an excellent opportunity to get to know the city and the people who live there and make valuable social connections.

Patrick Karban

Another tip for travelers who would like to save money is to take part in free walking tours. These tours are top-rated in many cities around the world. Although they are advertised as "free," it is customary to tip the guide at the end, but this can be adjusted to your budget. Such tours are a fantastic way to discover local stories and secret places without booking an expensive guided tour in advance.

It would be best to watch local directories and tourism websites, which often offer local discounts. City or tourist cards sometimes give you free or discounted access to several sights. In cities such as Vienna or Amsterdam, you can often use museums, sights, and even public transport for less with such cards, representing a considerable saving for budget-conscious travelers.

This is How Sarah Would Approach It

Sarah carefully planned her trip to Kyoto, taking into account various aspects such as transportation, accommodation, food, activities and additional expenses. Below is a detailed list of her expected expenses for the entire trip, including buffers and smaller purchases such as a luggage scale and packing cubes.

1. Flight Costs:

- Flight (outward and return flight): $ 700

- Additional costs for checked baggage (46 pounds): $ 50
  Total cost for flights: $ 750

2. Accommodation Costs:

- Airbnb Ryokan (7 nights): $ 110 per night

- Discount for more extended stays: 10 %
  Total cost of accommodation: $ 693

3. Catering:

- Breakfast: 7 days * $ 10 = $ 70

- Lunch: 7 days * $ 20 = $ 140

- Dinner: 7 days * $ 30 = $ 210

- Snacks and drinks: 7 days * $ 8 = $ 56
  Total cost for meals: $ 476

4. Transportation On Site:

- Tourist ticket (7 days): $ 25

- Rental car (2 days): $ 100

- Gasoline costs: $ 30
  Total cost of transportation: $ 155

5. Activities and Entrance Fees:

- Entrance fees for temples and palaces: $ 75

- Traditional tea ceremony: $ 40

- Other activities (boat trip, spontaneous excursions): $ 50
  Total cost of activities: $ 165

6. Further Acquisitions:

- Suitcase scale: $ 15

- Packing cubes: $ 30
  Total cost of equipment: $ 45

7. Various Expenses and Buffers:

Patrick Karban

- buffer (approx. 10 % of the total budget): $ 200

Total budget for the trip:

- Flights: $ 750

- Accommodation: $ 693

- Catering: $ 476

- Transportation: $ 155

- Activities: $ 165

- Equipment: $ 45

- Buffer: $ 200
  Total budget for the trip: $ 2,484

To make it easier to do the math and remember the figure, she rounded it up to an even $ 2,500.

Sarah decided to use the Trabee Pocket app during the trip to monitor her spending in real time and ensure she stayed within her budget. This app helped her break down her expenditures by category and identify trends if she was spending more than planned in certain areas.

In addition, she had planned 15% of her total budget as a buffer to cover unexpected expenses or emergencies. She felt well prepared and enjoyed her trip without financial stress.

Chapter 9: Efficient Time Management On The Go

Time management is essential to make the most of your travel experience. Working professionals and avid travelers can benefit from intelligent strategies to help them structure their daily activities, reduce stress and experience a more fulfilling trip. By implementing various techniques, travelers can ensure that their trips are both productive and enjoyable, allowing them to see more sights, have more experiences and reduce the chaos often associated with travel. This chapter is about practical methods for optimizing your schedule and maximizing every moment of your trip.

In this section, you will learn how to create a daily plan by dividing the time, prioritizing the sights and grouping similar activities. You'll also learn how important it is to research thoroughly, plan destinations and schedule breaks and downtime to have a balanced experience. We will also look at using digital planners and travel apps to simplify organization and cope with unexpected changes. These tools and strategies will improve travel efficiency and help you stay motivated and productive in new places. By the end of this chapter, you will be well-equipped with tips to improve your time management on the road and ensure a smooth and enjoyable travel experience.

Create a Daily Travel Plan

Creating a detailed itinerary that covers every stage of your door-to-door journey is crucial to making the most of your time and avoiding unnecessary stress. Well-structured planning that starts at home and lasts until your return will help you minimize travel times and ensure you make the most of your time on site.

Preparation for Departure

The first step begins even before the actual journey: Think about how you will get from your home to the airport or train station. There are several options available to you here. In addition to public transport or transportation services such as Uber or Bolt, you can consider driving your private car to the airport. This gives you more flexibility regarding departure times and eliminates dependency on timetables. Find out in advance about parking options at the airport - many offer long-term parking or even early booking discounts, which can reduce the cost of parking. Using airport transfer services is also stress-free, especially for larger baggage volumes or early flights.

As soon as you have made your travel arrangements, plan the times for check-in, security checks and any waiting times at the airport. A good guideline is to be at the airport about two hours before departure for international flights and 90 minutes before domestic flights. Please note that there may be longer waiting times on busy days or public holidays, so you should allow extra time. Apps like TripIt or Google Travel can help you keep track of flight dates, check-in times and boarding and give you timely reminders of when you should be on your way.

Arrival at the Location

After arriving at your destination, efficiently planning the route to your accommodation is essential. You can choose between public transportation, cabs, shuttle services or a rental car, depending on availability and convenience. A rental car could be an attractive option, especially if you want to visit many sights outside the city center or your destination is a more rural area. With the help of apps such as Rentalcars.com or Skyscanner, you can find cheap rental cars in advance and save time when picking them up. If you decide to use public transport, check the timetables and buy tickets in advance to avoid waiting times. Tools such as Google Maps or Citymapper help you plan the best transportation routes and get real-time information about departures and arrival times.

Paths Between the Destinations

When planning your daily activities, you should carefully calculate the distances between your destinations. It is essential to consider the time you spend at the sights and the arrival and transition times. This is particularly important in cities or regions with heavy traffic or long distances. A rental car can also be helpful here, especially if you want to get to places outside the city that are difficult to reach by public transport. Use real-time traffic information in Google Maps, Waze or local traffic apps to avoid traffic delays or rush hours.

Alternatively, in urban areas, you can often use public transportation or even bicycles, which are available for rent in many places. Some cities offer special tourist tickets or rental bikes, an inexpensive and flexible way to explore the city. Always plan enough buffer time between activities for possible delays or unexpected discoveries. A good rule of thumb is to leave at least 15-20 minutes of buffer time between activities or transportation to react flexibly to changes.

Structuring the Daily Activities

An effective way to organize your daily activities is to divide them into blocks of time. Assign a specific time frame to each activity, including arrival and departure times. Start your day with the most

145

important goals while fresh and energetic. Important sights such as famous museums or historical sites are best visited in the morning to avoid the crowds. Apps like Google Maps or Rome2Rio can help you plan the best routes between destinations and minimize transport time.

However, how you structure your day depends very much on the nature of your trip:

On a city trip, for example, to Paris or Rome, planning to visit major sights such as the Eiffel Tower or the Colosseum in the morning to avoid the rush hour is advisable. The afternoon can then be used to visit quieter places such as parks or charming districts like Montmartre or Trastevere. When traveling in cities, efficiently planning the routes between the sights is essential, as traffic in large cities is often an obstacle. Apps such as Citymapper or Moovit can help you quickly find the best route by public transport and minimize waiting times.

On adventure trips, such as hiking in the mountains or a road trip through Iceland, you should plan your most physically demanding activities for the middle of the day, when the temperatures are more pleasant, and the light conditions are optimal. Start your day early to set off on hikes or trips to remote destinations and plan enough buffer time for breaks or spontaneous photo stops. It is also essential to keep an eye on weather and road conditions. Apps such as Waze or unique weather apps help check current conditions and adapt flexibly.

The daily schedule is often more relaxed on a relaxing vacation in a beach resort or a quiet area. Here, you can spread your most important activities, such as beach visits or spa treatments, flexibly throughout the day. Plan more time for breaks and rest, as the focus is on relaxation. Walking in the surrounding area or visiting a local market can offer interesting diversions while prioritizing relaxation. Here, too, Google Maps can help you find quiet places or cozy restaurants off the beaten track.

Remember to integrate meals and breaks into your plan. It's tempting to plan as many activities as possible, but without breaks, you could quickly become exhausted and lose the fun of the trip. Plan your meals strategically by looking for restaurants or cafés near your sights in advance to avoid waiting times and unnecessary wandering. If possible, book in advance to make the most of your time. Good time management also considers buffer times to allow for spontaneous explorations and unforeseen delays.

Travel Planning Tools and Apps

Digital tools are a great help when organizing and navigating your trip efficiently. TripIt and Google Travel collect all your booking data and travel documents in one place and offer you reminders and notifications so that you can keep track of your travel schedule. With Google Maps or Citymapper, you can plan routes, call up real-time traffic information, and find alternative routes if traffic is heavier than expected. These apps also allow you to save offline maps to navigate quickly, even without an internet connection.

If you want to rent a car, apps such as Rentalcars.com or Kayak can help you find cheap rental options. They often offer comparisons between different providers so that you can find the best deal. Especially for rural or difficult-to-access regions, a rental car can be the ideal solution to be more flexible and not dependent on public transportation.

147

Consider External Factors

Local events such as public holidays, fairs or festivals can significantly impact your travel plan. Plan whether there are any significant events taking place during your travel period that could potentially lead to traffic disruptions or closed sights. Use platforms such as Timeanddate.com or Localholidays.com to take holidays or local specialties into account. It would be best if you also made sure that sights or museums are not inaccessible due to seasonal closures or maintenance work.

Maintain Flexibility

Even with detailed planning, you should always remain flexible. Buffer times between activities allow you to react to unforeseen delays without upsetting your daily schedule. A rule of thumb is to consider about 20% of your daily schedule as flexible. This allows you to make spontaneous discoveries or take unexpected breaks without stress.

With these detailed steps, you can create a well-planned itinerary that takes every aspect of your trip into account—from the moment you leave home to the moment you return. This ensures that you make the most of your time while leaving room for spontaneity and relaxation.

Allow Time for Transportation and Downtime

A balance between exploration and relaxation is essential to maintain energy during your trip. Planning buffer times between activities is vital to achieving this balance. This allows you to factor in unforeseen delays and reduce stress, making your travel plans more flexible and enjoyable. Buffer times ensure that you can focus on one sight at a time to enjoy the beauty of each place without feeling overwhelmed or exhausted.

Planned downtime is another effective strategy for maintaining your energy levels. Whether you visit a cozy café, relax by the pool at your accommodation or take a walk through a quiet park - these relaxing moments can recharge your batteries. A time-out does not mean you are wasting precious travel time, but a necessary break to regenerate yourself and your body. When planning your itinerary, you should allow time for such relaxing breaks so that you have enough time to unwind.

You must also know exactly what your energy level is and choose strenuous activities accordingly. Everyone has different peak times throughout the day. Some people are full of energy in the morning. In contrast, others may feel more active in the afternoon or evening. Plan your most physically demanding and adventurous activities, such as hiking or sightseeing, during peak energy times. Conversely, you should plan less strenuous activities such as museum visits or leisurely walks if you are tired. If you harmonize your activities with your natural energy rhythm, you can enjoy them better and avoid a breakdown.

Using the transition times productively can significantly improve your travel experience. The time you spend on planes, trains, buses or even long car journeys should be well spent. Instead, you can use this time to focus on things that will help you on your way. Reading a book about your next destination can give you better insights and improve your understanding. If you keep a travel diary, you can document your experiences, reflect on the day's events and plan future activities. Alternatively, you can use the transition period to sort through photos or prepare the next few days so your trip is well structured and you don't feel rushed.

149

Planned buffer times play a decisive role in effective time management when traveling. Unexpected delays are common, such as traffic jams or meals that take longer than expected. You can compensate for these delays with built-in buffer times without drastically affecting your schedule. For example, suppose you are planning a city tour followed by a visit to a famous museum. In that case, you can allow an hour or two buffer time between the two activities to ensure that the museum visit fits in time due to unforeseen circumstances. This approach reduces stress and ensures that every activity can be thoroughly enjoyed without rushing.

Planned downtimes should be taken into account. These are opportunities to come into contact with the local culture in a relaxed atmosphere. A visit to a local café allows you to relax and immerse yourself in the everyday life of the destination. Sipping a coffee while watching the locals or chatting with the barista will give you unique insights into the culture you might miss on standardized tours. The time you spend in your accommodation, for example, reading in the garden or enjoying a spa service, is also a welcome change from a packed itinerary.

Using Apps and Tools for Time Management

Efficient time management is crucial for an optimal travel experience in today's fast-paced world. An effective strategy to implement this is using technical aids to optimize travel plans and maintain an overview. With the advent of smartphones and apps, travelers can plan every trip down to the last detail, ensuring they get the most out of their journey.

Travel planning apps like TripIt are invaluable for planning itineraries and getting real-time updates. Imagine having all your travel data, such as flights, hotel bookings and car rentals, in one place. TripIt Pro, for example, updates its notifications to inform users when they should leave for the airport based on current traffic conditions (TripIt: Travel Planner, 2023). This forward-thinking approach helps travelers avoid unnecessary stress and ensures seamless transitions between the various stages of the journey.

Setting up alarms and reminders for important events is another essential way to be on time and not miss any activities. Whether it's a business meeting, a dinner reservation or a city tour, timely notifications will keep you on track. Integrating these reminders into your daily schedule allows you to manage your time better and avoid waiting times. If you set up automatic notifications, busy professionals and travel enthusiasts can ensure they receive all the essential information.

Using time tracking tools is another great way to monitor travel time and make any necessary adjustments. Apps designed for time management can provide information on how long different activities take so that travelers can improve their schedules. A tool like Toggl can divide your day into sections and show you where time is used well and where it could be used better. This approach increases productivity and ensures a balanced mix of activities and relaxation.

Navigation apps such as Google Maps are indispensable for finding your way around unfamiliar places. These apps offer more than just directions. They provide real-time traffic information, public transportation options, and walking routes. Google Maps offers a variety of functions for researching travel destinations and efficient navigation under the umbrella name Google Travel (The Best Travel Apps for 2022, n.d.). Such functions can save you valuable time you would otherwise have to determine the best routes manually. In addition, understanding the current traffic situation

151

can help travelers avoid delays and choose alternative routes if necessary. You can also use Google Maps to calculate the distance between two destinations, displaying the estimated journey time. This helps to check whether the planned schedule makes sense.

In addition, Rome2Rio is a great app that helps you compare different transportation options worldwide. With Rome2Rio, you can quickly determine whether it is best to fly between two destinations, take the train, hire a car or use public transport. The app also shows you the approximate costs for each option, which makes it particularly useful if you are planning a route with multiple modes of transportation. This allows you to find not only the fastest but also the cheapest option for your journey.

If you mainly want to get around a city by public transport, Moovit is an indispensable app. It provides real-time information on bus, train and metro timetables in over 3,000 cities worldwide. Moovit shows you the fastest route, the best connections and even when you need to get off. This app is handy if you are in large cities and rely on local transportation. It offers a reliable way to ensure you arrive at your destinations on time.

Making sensible use of these options can significantly improve both the planning phase and the realization of your trip. For example, everything will work smoothly if you use TripIt to manage all your reservations or even TripIt Pro to notify you of changed flight times or terminal gates. So you no longer have to rummage through emails or printed pages to find your itinerary. Setting up alarms on your smartphone can act as a second layer of security and ensure that you stick to your schedule.

Another significant advantage of Google Maps is the ability to find places. This makes it very easy to find a restaurant, ATM or petrol station nearby, especially when traveling. You can also use it to get reviews and recommendations and quickly decide where to eat or which sights to visit. These navigation tools ensure that potential obstacles are avoided and that every part of the journey is fun.

With the combination of Google Maps, Rome2Rio, Moovit and TripIt, you have the tools to not only plan your itinerary in detail but also to react flexibly to changes and always choose the best transportation option. This allows you to make the most of your time and efficiently reach every stop on your journey.

This is How Sarah Would Approach It

Based on the tips in this chapter and her previous tips and planning, Sarah now draws up the following itinerary for her trip to Kyoto:

Day 1: Departure and arrival in Kyoto

- **06:00 am**: Departure from home to the airport by cab.

- **06:45 AM**: Arrival at the airport, check-in and security check.

- **08:30 AM**: Boarding the flight to Tokyo.

- **09:00 AM**: Departure for Tokyo.

- **02:30 PM (local time Japan)**: Arrival in Tokyo. Sarah uses the time for a short break and a snack at the airport.

- **04:30 PM**: Onward flight to Osaka.

- **06:00 PM**: Arrival in Osaka. Sarah takes the Shinkansen (express train) to Kyoto.

- **06:30 PM**: Departure from Osaka Airport to Kyoto (Shinkansen).

- **07:15 PM**: Arrival at Kyoto Station.

- **07:30 PM**: Sarah takes a cab to her accommodation in the Gion district (about a 15-minute drive).

- **07:45 PM**: Check-in at the Airbnb Ryokan.

- **08:15 PM**: Dinner at the Tempura Endo Yasaka restaurant (close to the Gion district, approx. 10 minutes on foot).

- **09:30 PM**: Return to the accommodation, time to relax.

Day 2: Discover Kyoto's temples and gardens

- **07:30 AM**: Breakfast at Arabica Kyoto Higashiyama (5 minutes' walk).

- **08:00 AM**: Visit a supermarket or FamilyMart (5-minute walk) to buy snacks and drinks.

- **08:45 AM**: Departure to Fushimi Inari Shrine (approx. 25 minutes by train from Gion Shijo Station to Inari Station).

- **09:15 AM**: Arrive at Fushimi Inari Shrine and walk through the famous Torii gates.

- **12:00 PM**: Lunch at the Vermillion Café near the shrine.

- **01:30 PM**: Drive to Kiyomizu-dera Temple (approx. 20 minutes by cab).

- **02:00 PM**: Arrival and exploration of the temple.

- **04:00 PM**: Walk through the Gion district and visit a traditional tea house (Ippodo Tea).

- **06:00 PM**: Return to the accommodation, break.

- **07:30 PM**: Dinner at the Gion Kappa restaurant (10 minutes' walk).

- **09:00 PM**: Return to the accommodation.

Day 3: Culture and history

- **08:00 AM**: Breakfast at Kissako Kyogoku (5 minutes' walk).

- **09:00 AM**: Departure by subway (Karasuma Line) to Kyoto Imperial Palace (approx. 30 minutes ride).

- **09:30 AM**: Guided tour of the palace.

- **12:00 PM**: Lunch at Omen Kyoto near the palace (5 minutes on foot).

- **01:30 PM**: Walk along the Philosopher's Walk and visit the Nanzen-ji Temple.

- **04:00 PM**: Return to the accommodation, time to relax.

- **07:00 PM**: Dinner at Gion Mametora (a 10-minute walk), known for its kaiseki cuisine.

- **09:00 PM**: Return to the accommodation.

Day 4: Day trip to the surrounding area (with rental car)

- **07:30 AM**: Breakfast in the accommodation.

Patrick Karban

- **08:00 AM**: Pick up the rental car from the Toyota Rent a Car Kyoto Ekimae rental station (approx. 10 minutes by cab).

- **09:00 AM**: Departure toward Kameoka for a hike (approx. 45-minute drive).

- **10:00 AM**: Arrival in Kameoka, hike in the Hozu Gorge.

- **01:00 PM**: Lunch at Soba-no-Sato (famous for soba noodles).

- **03:00 PM**: Return to Kyoto (45 minutes drive).

- **04:00 PM**: Return to the accommodation, short break.

- **06:00 PM**: Return of the rental car at Toyota Rent a Car Kyoto Ekimae.

- **07:30 PM**: Dinner at Hyotei (3 Michelin stars, known for kaiseki cuisine).

- **09:30 PM**: Return to the accommodation.

Day 5: Bamboo Grove and tea ceremony

- **07:30 AM**: Breakfast in a café.

- **08:30 AM**: Departure to Arashiyama (approx. 25 minutes by train from Gion-Shijo Station to Saga-Arashiyama Station).

- **09:00 AM**: Visit the Arashiyama bamboo forest and the Tenryu-ji temple.

- **12:00 PM**: Lunch at Shoraian, specializing in tofu dishes.

- **01:30 PM**: Attend a traditional ceremony at the Camellia Tea House near the Kiyomizu-dera.

- **04:00 PM**: Return to the accommodation, short break.

- **07:00 PM**: Dinner at the Gion Tanto restaurant, famous for its okonomiyaki.

- **09:00 PM**: Return to the accommodation.

Day 6: Cultural Discoveries and Jidai Matsuri

- **07:30 AM**: Breakfast in the accommodation.

- **09:00 AM**: Visit to the Kinkaku-ji (Golden Pavilion). Arrival by bus (approx. 35 minutes from Gion).

- **12:00 PM**: Lunch at Ryoanji Yudofu near Kinkaku-ji.

- **02:00 PM**: Participation in the Jidai Matsuri Festival in Kyoto.

- **05:00 PM**: Return to the accommodation, short break.

- **07:30 PM**: Dinner at Nishiki Warai (local specialties at the Nishiki market).

- **09:30 PM**: Return to the accommodation.

Day 7: Final explorations and return journey

- **08:00 AM**: Breakfast at the accommodation, packing and check-out.

- **09:00 AM**: On your last walk through Kyoto, visit the Nishiki market for souvenirs.

- **12:00 PM**: Lunch at Menya Inoichi (famous for ramen).

- **02:00 PM**: Departure by train to Osaka (Shinkansen).

- **03:00 PM**: Arrival at Osaka Airport, check-in and security check.

- **06:00 PM**: Return flight to Europe.

- **11:00 PM (local time Europe)**: Arrival in Europe, return journey home.

- **12:00 AM**: Arrival home, end of the journey.

Chapter 10: Overcoming Challenges When Traveling and Staying Healthy

Overcoming challenges when traveling and staying healthy are crucial for a successful and enjoyable trip. Dealing with issues such as travel fatigue and jet lag can make the difference between a smooth and stressful trip. If you take care of your health on the road, you can make the most of your travel experience and feel just as good, if not better, when you return than when you left. This chapter looks at the various methods of overcoming these common travel obstacles and offers practical advice and strategies for travelers of all kinds.

In this chapter, you will find tips on how to recognize and alleviate travel fatigue and jet lag symptoms so that you stay energized and focused on your travels. It also discusses how creating a comfortable travel environment and respecting sleep schedules can make the transition between time zones much more straightforward. It also explores strategies for implementing wellness routines, from physical activity to conscious food choices. The chapter also offers further insights into stress management through mindfulness practices and proper hydration. Finally, it addresses specific travel challenges, such as overcoming language barriers and ensuring personal safety, to provide a comprehensive offering for a smooth and healthy travel experience.

Dealing With Travel Fatigue and Jet Lag

Dealing effectively with travel fatigue and jet lag is essential for a smooth journey. Early recognition of symptoms is crucial in mitigating the effects of these common travel problems. Symptoms such as drowsiness, irritability and difficulty concentrating can often be minimized by timely measures such as adequate hydration,

159

strategic naps and exercise. Staying hydrated is essential; having a water bottle to hand and drinking plenty helps to combat the dehydration that often accompanies long flights and climate changes.

Another essential strategy is to prepare for possible delays. Flight delays and long layovers can increase mental stress when traveling, so it is necessary to create a comfortable environment. Take a neck pillow, noise-canceling headphones, an eye mask and small snacks with you to make yourself comfortable while you wait. These things provide physical comfort and reduce stress by helping you to stay relaxed despite the circumstances.

A gradual change in your sleep rhythm before departure can make the transition to a new time zone much more accessible. You can adjust your bedtime by about an hour every day before your trip. A good night's sleep before the trip ensures your body is well-rested and can cope better with the disruption. Avoiding alcohol and caffeine before and during the flight contributes to a better recovery, as these substances can affect the sleep rhythm and water balance.

Exposure to light is another effective method of overcoming jet lag. Light is an essential signal for your body's internal clock, and the right timing can help you align your circadian rhythm with the local time at your destination. Exposing yourself to natural daylight when you arrive signals to your body that it's time to wake up and get active, reducing fatigue when you change time zones. Conversely, avoiding bright lights and screens before bedtime helps you to sleep better.

If used strategically, short naps can alleviate travel fatigue and jet lag. A 20-30-minute nap can regenerate your energy without causing tiredness or disturbing your night's sleep. However, it is important to avoid napping too close to bedtime, as this could make it difficult to fall asleep later.

Regular exercise while riding is essential to maintain blood circulation and avoid stiffness. Standing up to stretch, walking down the aisle or even doing simple exercises in your seat can make a big difference. Exercise keeps your muscles active and reduces the risk of deep vein thrombosis (DVT) on long flights.

Creating a comfortable travel environment goes beyond packing the right equipment. This includes planning your itinerary so that you have as little stress as possible. You can choose flights that suit your usual sleeping patterns. For example, if you are flying overnight, you should book a flight where you can sleep during your regular waking hours. After your arrival, you will integrate into the everyday life of the locals by eating your meals at the correct times and participating in activities that correspond to the regional schedule.

A smooth travel experience also includes paying attention to what you eat and drink. Eat light meals that are easy to digest, as heavy meals can make you feel sluggish and unwell. Drink herbal teas, which can have a calming effect. At the same time, avoid sugary snacks, as they can lead to fluctuating energy levels.

In addition to these strategies, technology can help combat travel fatigue and jet lag. Various apps adapt light exposure and sleep rhythm to your travel route. Such apps can tell you when to look for light and when to avoid it to maximize the effectiveness of this measure.

Finally, consulting a doctor's practice before embarking on a long journey can provide additional support. Please discuss whether you can take supplements such as melatonin, which can regulate your sleep-wake cycle, if you take the correct dose. Medical advice

161

ensures the chosen products are safe and suitable for your health needs. However, it is essential to remember that over-the-counter sleeping pills can only mask the symptoms and have unwanted side effects. A doctor can help you find the best course of action for your particular situation.

Maintain Wellness Routines When Traveling

Maintaining your well-being while traveling can be challenging, but keeping your physical and mental health in mind is crucial. To enjoy the travel experience to the full, it is helpful to focus on a holistic wellness routine that involves both the body and the mind.

Physical Health While Traveling

Staying physically active is a good starting point to promote your well-being. Exercise helps to keep the circulation going and prevent tiredness. You can explore new cities by going for walks or hikes, improving your health and intensifying the travel experience. Many destinations offer guided hikes where you can discover cultural and historical sights at the same time. If you stay in a hotel, you should use the fitness facilities there. Many hotels have treadmills, weights and sometimes even swimming pools to help you stay fit.

If your hotel or accommodation doesn't have a gym, workout apps can be a great alternative. These apps offer a variety of exercises, from high-intensity interval training (HIIT) to yoga, which you can do right in your room. Short but regular workouts can help you feel active even on the go. Yoga or stretching exercises are beneficial to relieve tension after long flights or long days on your feet.

Healthy Nutrition On The Go

Healthy eating often requires more planning when traveling, but it pays off. Favor meals that contain fruit, vegetables and lean protein to provide your body with the nutrients it needs. Local markets often offer fresh fruit and vegetables that you can use for quick, nutritious snacks. When eating out, choose grilled or baked dishes instead of fried foods. You can also ask for dressings and sauces to be added to better control your calorie intake.

Pre-planned meals can help save time and ensure balanced choices. Research restaurants that offer healthy options or meet special dietary requirements. Healthy snacks such as nuts, dried fruit or wholemeal bars are also handy companions to avoid cravings on the go and prevent impulsive, unhealthy eating decisions.

Mental Well-Being and Stress Management

Your mental well-being should not be neglected when traveling, either. Although traveling offers an exciting opportunity to discover new places and break out of your daily routine, it can also be exhausting as your usual routines are disrupted, and you must adapt to a new environment. A conscious digital time-out can help to reduce travel stress and increase your focus on positive experiences. By setting fixed times to check emails or use social media, you can use the rest of the day to consciously perceive your surroundings and enjoy what you have experienced without distractions. This promotes meatal relaxation and allows you to live more intensely in the moment and fully enjoy your travel experiences.

Mindfulness and relaxation exercises also play an essential role in maintaining inner balance when traveling. For example, taking small breaks to read a book or do breathing exercises can help you

163

organize your thoughts and recharge your batteries. Being in nature – whether in a park, at the beach, or on a hike – offers a simple yet effective way to quiet your mind and recharge. Exercise in combination with fresh air is an effective way to combat stress and naturally relax your mind.

Hydration and Prevention

Hydration is an essential part of self-care, especially when traveling. Airplane cabins or hot climates can quickly lead to dehydration. Therefore, drink water regularly to maintain your fluid balance. Fruit and vegetables containing water, such as watermelon, cucumber or oranges, can also be a refreshing and nutrient-rich addition.

Preventive measures are essential, especially if you are susceptible to travel-related illnesses. According to the Centers for Disease Control and Prevention (CDC), up to 50% of travelers to developing countries contract the disease. Problems such as heatstroke or parasite infections can severely impair the travel experience. Therefore, keep up to date with the necessary vaccinations and health precautions and pack a first-aid kit with the most essential medicines such as antiseptics, plasters and remedies for typical ailments.

Sun Protection and Self-Care

If you are traveling to sunny climes, sun protection is critical. Apply sunscreen with a high sun protection factor (SPF) regularly and renew it, especially after swimming. Also, protect yourself from harmful UV rays with clothing, sunglasses and hats. This significantly reduces the risk of sunburn and long-term skin damage.

Don't forget that mental health is just as important as physical well-being. Traveling can change routines, and the new impressions can be overwhelming. Therefore, plan targeted relaxation phases to give your mind and body space to recover.

Tips for Dealing with Special Travel Challenges

Overcoming language barriers and cultural misunderstandings is crucial for a smooth travel experience. Understanding and effectively overcoming these challenges can turn potentially frustrating situations into valuable experiences. This is how you can achieve this:

Start by learning basic phrases in the local language. Simple greetings like "Hello" and "Thank you" and essential questions like "How much?" or "Where...?" can make a big difference. These expressions facilitate communication and show respect and appreciation for the local culture. According to The Curious Sparrow, knowing the most essential words helps with interactions such as shopping, ordering in restaurants and paying bills (The Curious Sparrow, 2022). Offline translation apps such as DeepL or Duolingo can also be downloaded. These apps can provide instant translations and even help with pronunciation, which is invaluable in places where English is not widely spoken.

Every culture has customs and manners that may differ significantly from what you are used to. For example, non-verbal communication plays a vital role in many cultures. Some gestures that have a harmless meaning in one country can be offensive in another. By observing locals and adapting your behavior

Patrick Karban

accordingly, you can avoid misunderstandings and show cultural sensitivity. In some cultures, a smile is seen as inviting; in others, it is not. The same applies to gestures such as a thumbs-up or a nod. Researching these aspects is always helpful to find your way in social interactions.

You can use maps, navigation apps and tips for public transport when exploring unfamiliar areas. Apps like Google Maps can guide you through unfamiliar streets. In contrast, local transport apps can provide up-to-date information on routes and timetables. You can familiarize yourself with the city's layout and transport system. If you know which bus or train to take, you can save time and reduce stress. It can also be helpful to have a physical card with you as a backup in case the technology fails, or you are in areas with limited internet access.

We want to make sure that you are safe on your travels. Always be aware of your surroundings and keep your valuables close to you. Use theft-proof bags and carry belt pouches to protect important documents and cash. You can avoid unnecessary trouble if you are informed about the local laws. In some countries, for example, strict regulations exist for taking photographs in certain situations or for the dress code at religious sites. If you understand these rules in advance, you can avoid unintentional violations.

Finding out in advance about illnesses or dietary restrictions in the local language can also be life-saving. This ensures that you can pass on important information, especially in emergencies or when going out to eat. If it is easily accessible, this information can prevent dangerous situations for travelers with allergies or special health needs.

Another effective strategy is the use of visual aids. If language barriers seem impossible, don't hesitate to use pictures, drawings or gestures to convey your message. Showing a picture of a landmark or an object you are looking for can often bridge the gap better than words alone could. This method works like a game of charades. Nevertheless, it is a practical method of communication if you don't know the correct vocabulary.

Another powerful tool is the Google Translate camera function, which allows you to translate text using your phone's camera in real-time. This function can be helpful for understanding menus, signs and instructions only available in the local language. You can download the languages you need offline, so you don't have to rely on an internet connection.

You can always ask questions instead of making assumptions. If in doubt, the polite question "Do you speak English?" in the local language can open the door. People are often more willing to help if they see that you are trying to communicate respectfully. If you speak slowly and clearly and use simple vocabulary, you can avoid misunderstandings and ensure your message is understood.

Traveling to a foreign country always brings challenges, and the language barriers can be challenging. Patience and a good sense of humor can go a long way. Misunderstandings will happen, but they are part of the experience and can lead to unexpected and rewarding encounters.

Travel Insurance Options and Emergency Contacts/Resources

To ensure a safe and stress-free trip, you must protect yourself financially and know what you can do in an emergency. Choosing the right travel insurance is one of the most critical steps in achieving this goal. First, consider your requirements, the nature of your trip, the activities you want to participate in and any pre-

167

existing medical conditions. Travel insurance policies vary considerably, so knowing exactly what each policy covers and what is excluded is essential. Some policies do not cover high-risk activities such as skiing, diving, mountaineering or pre-existing conditions unless this is explicitly mentioned. Read the small print carefully and contact your insurance company if anything is unclear.

Typical travel insurance policies include:

- Travel health insurance: Covers medical emergencies abroad. This is particularly important as many health insurance companies do not cover costs outside the home country.

- Travel cancellation insurance: Refunds costs if you cannot travel for unforeseen reasons (e.g., illness).

- Luggage insurance: Protects against loss, theft or damage to luggage.

Also, check whether the insurance covers emergency repatriation if you must be flown back to your home country in the event of illness. This is particularly important when traveling to regions with limited access to medical care.

One of your top priorities should be a comprehensive list of local emergency numbers, embassy contacts and travel assistance services. You can often find this information online or in travel guides for your destination. Keep these contacts easily accessible digitally on your cell phone or in a notebook. Embassies can provide valuable support in emergencies such as a medical problem or the loss of your passport.

Another important preparatory step is to research medical facilities at your destination. Find hospitals, clinics and pharmacies that are known to treat international patients and may understand the language you speak. Apps like TripWhistle Global SOS help you find local emergency numbers and get directions to nearby healthcare facilities. These apps often offer functions that allow you to share your location directly with emergency services in an emergency.

You should also always carry prescription medication for your trip and reserve a few extra days in case of delays. Keep this medication in your hand luggage to ensure that it does not get lost. It is also advisable to carry a copy of your prescriptions and a document from your doctor explaining your medical needs. This can help simplify the customs process and reorder the proper medication in an emergency.

It is also practical to save the local emergency numbers on your phone. Not all countries use the same emergency call system as Germany (112), so it is essential to know the relevant numbers for emergencies and the police and fire department at your destination. Share this information with fellow travelers so everyone knows how to act quickly in an emergency.

Many health insurance policies do not cover medical costs outside the home country, and particular plans such as Medicare in the USA do not cover treatment costs abroad. If necessary, check what your insurance covers and consider additional travel health insurance. This insurance can help give you peace of mind in a medical emergency without burdening you financially. Always keep your medication in the original, labeled packaging to avoid possible complications at customs.

Patrick Karban

Vaccinations and Travel Preparation

Vaccinations are central to travel health and should be planned well in advance. Many vaccinations take several weeks to take full effect, so you should make an appointment with your doctor at least 6-8 weeks before your trip to ensure you receive all the necessary vaccinations on time. Specific vaccination requirements may vary depending on your destination, so it is essential to find out in advance which vaccinations are required or recommended for your destination.

Some vaccinations, such as tetanus, polio, or hepatitis, must be regularly refreshed. It is advisable to keep these vaccinations up to date, even if they are not explicitly required for your destination. Vaccinations such as yellow fever are required for travel to certain tropical or subtropical countries. In such cases, you will need an international vaccination certificate (the so-called Yellow Card), which you must present when entering the country.

In addition to vaccinations, malaria prevention or other preventive measures may also be necessary, depending on where you are traveling. Your doctor or a tropical medicine specialist can help you choose the best protection for your destination. It is vital to plan these medical precautions early to ensure your body has enough time to react to the vaccinations and develop comprehensive protection.

This is How Sarah Would Approach It

Having planned her trip to Kyoto in detail, Sarah considered all aspects of health and safety to ensure a smooth and enjoyable journey. Here is her approach based on the aspects covered in Chapter 10 that are relevant to her trip to Kyoto.

1. Dealing With Jet Lag and Travel Fatigue

As Sarah traveled from Europe to Japan, she was aware of the potential effects of jet lag and travel fatigue. To make the transition to the new time zone easier, she had already adjusted her sleeping pattern before she left. By shifting her bedtimes about an hour earlier each day, she could better cope with the time difference of several hours between Europe and Japan.

During the flight, she made sure to drink enough water and avoid caffeinated drinks and alcohol to prevent dehydration and sleep disturbances. She also had melatonin tablets with her, which she used to regulate her sleep-wake cycle for the first few nights after her arrival, as recommended by her doctor. She also used the Timeshifter app to find the optimal light and sleep strategy and overcome her jet lag more quickly.

After arriving in Kyoto, she deliberately exposed herself to daylight. She tried to adapt to the local time as quickly as possible by remaining active during the day and only sleeping in the evening. To make long flights more comfortable, she also packed a neck pillow, a sleep mask and noise-canceling headphones so that she could relax during the flight.

2. Wellness Routines When Traveling

Sarah knew traveling could be exhausting, so she emphasized promoting her physical and mental health. She planned regular walks and hikes to stay fit, such as the walk along the Philosopher's Path or the hike through the Hozu Gorge. These activities helped her to keep moving while enjoying the beauty of Kyoto's nature and culture.

171

Sarah also used yoga apps for light stretching exercises in her accommodation to relieve tension after long days or flights. It was essential for her to maintain healthy eating habits. She prioritized fresh local ingredients such as vegetables and fish, abundantly available in Japan. Local markets like the Nishiki market offered an excellent opportunity to buy fresh snacks to stay healthy on the go.

Mental health was also essential to Sarah. She consciously took time for mindfulness by carrying a small book with her every day to record her impressions. She also made sure not to use any electronic devices in the evening before bed to help her calm down and relax.

3. Travel Insurance and Emergency Precautions

Sarah planned her trip with comfort and safety in mind. She took out comprehensive travel health insurance that covered medical emergencies and possible repatriation. As she wanted long-term preparation, she had ensured that her insurance would also cover treatment in Japan and that medical emergencies would be covered without any problems.

She also saved the German embassy's emergency numbers and contact details in Kyoto on her phone so she could react quickly in an emergency. She also used the TripWhistle Global SOS app to find emergency numbers and medical facilities nearby.

4. Health Preparation and Vaccinations

Sarah had informed herself in advance about all the medical requirements for Japan and ensured that her standard vaccinations (such as tetanus, diphtheria and hepatitis) were up to date. Although

Japan is not a high-risk area for tropical diseases, she had her first-aid kit with her, which included essential medicines, such as painkillers, antihistamines and disinfectants, in case of an emergency.

She also always carried sunscreen with a high sun protection factor to protect herself from the intense autumn sun during her hikes. She also ensured she always had enough water to avoid dehydration.

5. Dealing With Cultural Differences and Safety

Sarah was aware that she was traveling in a different cultural context and made an effort to adapt to the local dress code and rules of conduct. She always wore long sleeves and covered shoulders, especially when visiting temples such as the Fushimi Inari and the Kiyomizu-dera. This showed her respect for local customs and helped her to avoid unpleasant situations.

Sarah also paid attention to her safety. She used a theft-proof bag for her valuables and left essential documents, such as her passport, in the safe at her accommodation. She only carried the bare essentials during her trips and used a money belt for cash and credit cards.

By consciously addressing cultural differences and preparing for medical emergencies, Sarah felt well-equipped to enjoy her trip to Kyoto safely and soundly.

Patrick Karban

Conclusion

This book offers a comprehensive and practical guide for travelers who want to use their time efficiently and overcome challenges while traveling effortlessly. With a clear focus on structure, health and safety, it guides the reader step-by-step through the various stages of a trip—from detailed planning to maintaining well-being on the road. It becomes clear that every trip should not only be well organized but also flexible so that they can react to unforeseen events.

The clever use of modern technologies, such as travel apps and digital tools, enables the reader to optimize travel planning and minimize stress. In addition to the practical application of tools, essential topics such as health care, language barriers and emergencies are also addressed and dealt with in detail.

Sarah's example runs through the book and illustrates how the theoretical concepts can be applied in practice. This combination of theory and practice makes the book particularly valuable for busy professionals, adventurers and anyone who wants to organize their trip efficiently and stress-free. The book covers everything travelers need for a safe, healthy and enjoyable journey with clear instructions, helpful tips and various valuable resources.

Why Sarah's journey will be successful

Sarah has planned her trip to Kyoto in detail and carefully to prepare well for all challenges. Her preparations cover all the essential areas, and a structured approach will ensure that her trip runs smoothly and provides her with unforgettable experiences.

Sarah is aware of the potential effects of jet lag and travel fatigue. By gradually adjusting her sleep rhythm before departure, she has already taken steps to make the change of time zones easier. During the flight, she drank plenty of water and avoided caffeinated drinks and alcohol to prevent dehydration. With apps such as *Timeshifter* and melatonin tablets, she has developed a strategy to combat jet lag effectively. This shows that she is well prepared for the physical challenge of a long journey.

Her wellness routines ensure that she stays healthy and fit while traveling. Regular walks and hikes, such as the Philosopher's Path or the Hozu Gorge, keep her physically active while experiencing the beauty of Kyoto's nature and culture. She also uses yoga apps to relieve tension after long days of traveling. Sarah pays attention to her diet by favoring fresh, local ingredients and carrying healthy snacks such as nuts or dried fruit. This keeps her energetic and healthy throughout the journey.

Sarah is also well-equipped for safety and emergency preparedness. She has taken out comprehensive travel health insurance that covers her in the event of a medical emergency in Japan and a possible repatriation. By storing emergency numbers and the contact details of the German embassy in her phone, she has ensured that she can act quickly in an emergency. Using apps such as *TripWhistle Global SOS* gives her additional security, knowing that she always has access to important medical facilities.

175

Sarah's attentiveness to cultural differences also contributes to the success of her trip. She respects local customs in Kyoto by dressing appropriately and respecting religious and cultural traditions. This adaptability helps her to avoid unpleasant situations and integrate smoothly into the local culture.

Through this thorough preparation, flexible planning and her conscious approach to health and safety, Sarah will find her trip stress-free and enriching. She is prepared for all eventualities and can concentrate on enjoying the beauty of Kyoto.

Reader Acknowledgement

Many thanks to all the readers who have embarked on this journey through the world of travel planning. Your efforts to improve your travel experiences are highly commendable, and I hope the information in this book will prove helpful in your future travels.

References

5 Ways to Use Social Media for Travel Planning. (n.d.). Travel Channel. Retrieved July 30, 2024, from https://www.travelchannel.com/interests/travel-tips/articles/use-social-media-to-plan-vacation

Exploring the World: Is Travel a Hobby? (n.d.). Marshmallow Challenge Blog. Retrieved July 30, 2024, from https://www.marshmallowchallenge.com/blog/exploring-the-world-is-travel-a-hobby/

Government of Canada, G. A. C. (2012, November 16). *Travel Advice and Advisories for Nigeria.* Travel.gc.ca. https://travel.gc.ca/destinations/nigeria

Helms, I. (2024, June 12). *New data highlights the importance of LGBTQ+-friendly destinations.* GayCities Wanderlust. https://www.gaycities.com/articles/89021/new-data-highlights-the-importance-of-lgbtq-friendly-destinations/

Step-by-Step Guide to Developing Your Own Travel Planner App. (n.d.). Solguruz.com. Retrieved July 30, 2024, from https://solguruz.com/blog/develop-a-travel-planner-app-like-tripit-and-wanderlog/

Team, P. (2023, August 30). *Seven Gen-Z travel trends transforming the hospitality industry.* Blog.pressreader.com. https://blog.pressreader.com/hotels/seven-gen-z-travel-trends-that-are-transforming-the-hospitality-industry

U.S. State Department Travel Advisories. (n.d.). InsureMyTrip. https://www.insuremytrip.com/travel-advice/travel-planning/us-state-dept-travel-advisories/

Welcome change: Travel and the LGBTQ community. (n.d.). Www.travelweekly.com. https://www.travelweekly.com/Travel-News/Travel-Agent-Issues/Welcome-change-Travel-LGBTQ-community

7 tips for planning a great travel itinerary to maximize your adventure. (n.d.). Www.gq.co.za. https://www.gq.co.za/culture/travel/7-tips-for-planning-a-great-travel-itinerary-to-maximise-your-adventure-717c8d09-681d-4e21-b9e4-aa9004a7396e

Brao, C. (2023, May 25). *Work Life Balance in the Summer: Maximizing Productivity and Enjoyment*. The Christopher Group. https://www.tcgco.com/work-life-balance-in-the-summer/

Career Contessa. (n.d.). *How to establish healthy boundaries at work*. Career Contessa. https://www.careercontessa.com/advice/healthy-boundaries-at-work/

How to craft a brilliant tour itinerary that your guests will rave about. (2024, February 13). Xola. https://www.xola.com/articles/tour-itinerary/

Iacurci, G. (2024, June 3). *5 ways to maximize your vacation days*. CNBC. https://www.cnbc.com/2024/06/03/here-are-some-ways-to-maximize-your-vacation-days.html

Indeed Editorial Team. (2023, August 31). *16 ways to set healthy boundaries at work*. Indeed Career Guide. https://www.indeed.com/career-advice/career-development/boundaries-at-work

Paulise, L. (n.d.). *Workation: Balancing Work And Vacation For Optimal Career Performance*. Forbes.

https://www.forbes.com/sites/lucianapaulise/2023/06/20/workation-balancing-work-and-vacation-for-optimal-career-performance/

PTO Hack: How to Maximize Vacation Days in 2024 - JoAnna E. (2023, October 28). Www.joannae.com. https://www.joannae.com/how-to-maximize-vacation-days/

Suni, E. (2021, February 5). *Jet lag: Symptoms: Causes, and How to Cope | Sleep Foundation.* Sleep Foundation. https://www.sleepfoundation.org/travel-and-sleep/jet-lag

Waterhouse, J. (2002, February 1). *Identifying some determinants of "jet lag" and its symptoms: a study of athletes and other travelers.* British Journal of Sports Medicine. https://doi.org/10.1136/bjsm.36.1.54

Connell, J., Page, S. J., & Meyer, D. (2015, February). *Visitor attractions and events: Responding to seasonality.* Tourism Management. https://doi.org/10.1016/j.tourman.2014.06.013

Five reasons why you should travel off-season | Projects Abroad. (n.d.). Www.projects-Abroad.org. https://www.projects-abroad.org/blog/why-travel-off-season/

Pröbstl-Haider, U., Hödl, C., Ginner, K., & Borgwardt, F. (2020, November). *Climate change: Impacts on outdoor activities in the summer and shoulder seasons.* Journal of Outdoor Recreation and Tourism. https://doi.org/10.1016/j.jort.2020.100344

Pitrelli, M. (2024, January 28). *How much does "shoulder season" travel save? We crunch the numbers in 5 top spots.* CNBC. https://www.cnbc.com/2024/01/29/how-much-does-shoulder-season-travel-save-we-crunched-the-numbers.html

US Department of Commerce, N. (n.d.). *Getting Traction: Tips for Traveling in Winter Weather.* Www.weather.gov. https://www.weather.gov/wrn/getting_traction

Understanding Off-Peak in the Travel Industry - Plantrip. (n.d.). Plantrip.io. https://plantrip.io/glossary/off-peak

Whitmore, G. (n.d.). *6 Severe Weather Safety Tips For Travelers.* Forbes. Retrieved July 30, 2024, from https://www.forbes.com/sites/geoffwhitmore/2024/05/17/6-tips-for-safe-travel-during-severe-weather/

Zhang, J., Yu, Z., Miao, C., Li, Y., & Qiao, S. (2022, February 18). *Cultural Tourism Weakens Seasonality: Empirical Analysis of Chinese Tourism Cities.* Country. https://doi.org/10.3390/land11020308

angelatravels. (2019, January 4). *The Best Outdoor Weather Forecasting Tips and Tools.* Angela Travels. https://angelatravels.com/the-best-outdoor-weather-forecasting-tips-and-tools/

Amazon.com | Compression Packing Cubes for Travel - Luggage and Backpack Organizer Packaging Cubes for Clothes (Dusty Teal and White, 2 Piece Set) | Packing Organizers. (2024). Amazon.com. https://www.amazon.com/Packing-Travel-Organizer-Compression-Carryon/dp/B078RSHPDP

BuyReviewer. (2024, May 24). *Efficient Travel Packing Tips.* Medium. https://medium.com/@buyreviewer/efficient-travel-packing-tips-562bf936793d

Elise, G. (2016, June 29). *Dressing Respectfully While Traveling in a Foreign Country.* Student Caffé Blog. http://blog.studentcaffe.com/dressing-respectfully-traveling-abroad/

Patrick Karban

How to Maximize Space as You're Packing. (2022, December 1). The New York Times. https://www.nytimes.com/wirecutter/guides/how-to-maximize-space-when-packing/

Jen. (2021, November 14). *10 Best Sustainable Travel Products - Green Packing Tips - Lens of Jen.* The Lens of Jen. https://www.lensofjen.org/my-top-10-sustainable-travel-products/

Packing Light - Eco Life Zone. (2023, December 9). https://www.ecolife.zone/packing-light

Tips for Choosing the Best Travel Bag. (n.d.). Rick Steves. Retrieved July 30, 2024, from https://www.ricksteves.com/travel-tips/packing-light/backpack-or-rolling-bag

Trip. (2024, February 7). *Dress Right: Visiting Different Cultures Respectfully.* https://tripjive.com/dress-right-visiting-different-cultures-respectfully/.

The Essential Travel Packing Checklist You Need Before any Trip. (2023, March 19). CABINZERO. https://www.cabinzero.com/blogs/packing-list/travel-packing-checklist

Wheeler, A. (2023, December 28). *The art of packing lightly: How to travel with just a cabin bag.* A Globe Well Traveled. https://aglobewelltravelled.com/2023/12/29/the-art-of-packing-lightly-how-to-fit-a-week-in-a-carry-on-bag/

Car sharing to help save the planet | Green City Times. (2017, December 20). Www.greencitytimes.com. https://www.greencitytimes.com/car-sharing/

Final Rule - Enhancing Transparency of Airline Ancillary Service Fees | US Department of Transportation. (2024).

Transportation.gov.
https://www.transportation.gov/airconsumer/ancillaryfeefinalrulea
pril2024

Federal Register :: Request Access. (n.d.).
Unblock.federalregister.gov.
https://www.federalregister.gov/documents/2022/10/20/2022-
22214/enhancing-transparency-of-airline-ancillary-service-fees

*How Sustainable Transportation Can Positively Impact the Future
- Edenred Benefits.* (2024, February 1). Edenredbenefits.com.
https://edenredbenefits.com/how-sustainable-transportation-can-
positively-impact-the-future/

How to Use Flight Price Alerts to Save Money on Your Next Trip.
(n.d.). Travel + Leisure. Retrieved July 30, 2024, from
https://www.travelandleisure.com/how-to-use-flight-price-alerts-
7644213

Langley, G. (2024, July 5). *How to Redeem Travel Credit Card
Points for Maximum Value.* The Lovers Passport.
https://theloverspassport.com/redeem-travel-credit-card-points-
maximum-value/

Pei, A. (2021, October 7). *5 Environmental Benefits of Sustainable
Transportation.* UCLA Transportation.
https://transportation.ucla.edu/blog/5-environmental-benefits-
sustainable-transportation

Steele, T. C., Jason. (2024, June 19). *Here are ways to find cheap
airfare when booking a flight.* The Points Guy.
https://thepointsguy.com/guide/strategies-to-find-cheap-airfare/

https://www.howstuffworks.com/about-author.htm. (2012, August
29). *Top 10 Alternative Transportation Methods.* HowStuffWorks.

Patrick Karban

https://science.howstuffworks.com/environmental/green-science/10-alternative-transportation-methods.htm

laponsie, maryalene. (2022, July 12). *How to maximize travel credit card rewards.* Cardratings.com. https://www.cardratings.com/travel/how-to-maximize-travel-credit-card-rewards.html

Baumgarten, M. (2021, November 10). *Hotels vs Hostels vs Airbnb.* Northeastern University Global Experience Office. https://geo.northeastern.edu/blog/hotels-vs-hostels-vs-airbnb/

Chan, I. C. C., Lam, L. W., Chow, C. W. C., Fong, L. H. N., & Law, R. (2017, September). *The effect of online reviews on hotel booking intention: The role of reader-reviewer similarity.* International Journal of Hospitality Management. https://doi.org/10.1016/j.ijhm.2017.06.007

Harms, N. (2016, October 15). *Pros and Cons: Hostel vs. hotel vs. Airbnb.* It's Not Hou It's Me. http://itsnothouitsme.com/2016/10/14/pros-and-cons-hostel-vs-hotel-vs-airbnb/

Norcross, A. (2022). *12 unconventional ways to save on travel. U.S. News & World Report.* Retrieved from https://travel.usnews.com/features/how-to-save-on-travel

Queer Adventurers. (2023, October 27). Queeradventurers.com. https://queeradventurers.com/hotel-safety-tips/

Roberts, T. (n.d.). *Eco Tourism: The Luxury Eco-Lodges Leading the Way.* Www.storylines.com. https://www.storylines.com/blog/eco-tourism-the-luxury-eco-lodges-leading-the-way

Tripadvisor. (2024). *The solo female traveler network - Tours for women - All you need to know BEFORE you go*. Retrieved from https://www.tripadvisor.com/Attraction_Review-g255100-d16875952-Reviews-The_Solo_Female_Traveler_Network_Tours_for_Women-Melbourne_Victoria.html

Tripadvisor. (2019, July 16). *Online Reviews Remain a Trusted Source of Information When Booking Trips, Reveals New Research | Tripadvisor*. Ir.tripadvisor.com. https://ir.tripadvisor.com/news-releases/news-release-details/online-reviews-remain-trusted-source-information-when-booking

Wright, J. (2023, July 19). *The 15 Best Eco Resorts in the World (2023)*. Bon Traveler. https://www.bontraveler.com/best-eco-resorts/

https://www.facebook.com/nomadicmatt. (2019, March 12). *Matthew Kepnes*. Nomadic Matt's Travel Site. https://www.nomadicmatt.com/travel-blogs/the-ultimate-guide-to-traveling-when-you-have-no-money/

7 Underrated Travel Planning Apps That Streamline Your Next Adventure. (n.d.). Mighty Travels Premium. Retrieved July 30, 2024, from https://www.mightytravels.com/2024/07/7-underrated-travel-planning-apps-that-streamline-your-next-adventure/

Authentic Travel. (n.d.). Local Travel. Retrieved July 30, 2024, from https://www.lokaltravel.com/discover-topic/authentic-travel

How to craft a brilliant tour itinerary that your guests will rave about. (2024, February 13). Xola. https://www.xola.com/articles/tour-itinerary/

Jewellery, O. T. M. (n.d.). *HOW TO AVOID TOURIST TRAPS AND SEEK AUTHENTIC ADVENTURES*. Off the Map Jewellery.

Patrick Karban

Retrieved July 30, 2024, from https://offthemapjewellery.com/blogs/off-the-map-blog/how-to-avoid-tourist-traps-and-seek-authentic-adventures

Jean-Louis, V. (2023, August 17). *25 Best Apps For Vacation Planning To Save Time and Money*. The Thought Card. https://thoughtcard.com/best-apps-for-vacation-planning/

Malichová, E., Straka, M., Buzna, Ľ., Scandolari, D., Scrocca, M., & Comerio, M. (2023, April 26). *Study of travelers' preferences towards travel offer categories and incentives in the journey planning context*. PLOS ONE. https://doi.org/10.1371/journal.pone.0284844

Nawijn, J., Marchand, M. A., Veenhoven, R., & Vingerhoets, A. J. (2010, February 10). *Vacationers Happier, but Most not Happier After a Holiday*. Applied Research in Quality of Life. https://doi.org/10.1007/s11482-009-9091-9

Roadtrippers Canada | Plan your journey, find amazing places, and take fascinating detours with the world's #1 roadtrip planning platform. (2018). Roadtrippers. https://roadtrippers.com/

Scott, S. (2022, June 11). *How to Keep Your Travel Itinerary Loose and Have an Incredible Vacation*. Wonder & Sundry. https://wonderandsundry.com/how-to-keep-your-travel-itinerary-loose-and-have-an-incredible-vacation/

Wanderlust, T. (2019, October 16). *27 of the world's secret destinations, as chosen by 27 experts*. Wanderlust. https://www.wanderlustmagazine.com/inspiration/27-secret-travel-destinations/

Average Vacation Costs in 2024. (2023, December 14). GOGO Charters. https://gogocharters.com/blog/average-vacation-cost/

BUDGET-FRIENDLY ORLANDO ACTIVITIES. (2021, November 1). Florida Citrus Sports. https://floridacitrussports.com/things-to-do/budget-friendly-orlando-activities/

Gravier, E. (2021, January 26). *Here are the best expense tracker apps of 2021*. CNBC. https://www.cnbc.com/select/best-expense-tracker-apps/

Holzhauer, B. (2021, May 26). *The Best Budgeting Apps Of June 2021*. Forbes Advisor. https://www.forbes.com/advisor/banking/best-budgeting-apps/

Papadimitriou, O. (n.d.). *4 Tips for Using Credit Cards Overseas*. Investopedia. https://www.investopedia.com/articles/pf/11/using-credit-cards-in-other-countries.asp

Rebecca, R. F. (2020, March 9). *Northern Florida Travel Guide: The Underrated, Adventurous Corner you Need to Explore*. Roam Free Rebecca. https://roamfreerebecca.com/nothern-florida-adventure/

The complete guide to business travel budgets. (n.d.). TravelPerk. https://www.travelperk.com/guides/budget-for-business-travel/

Wells, L. (2021, November 28). *Average Cost Of A Vacation: Transportation, Food, Entertainment*. Bankrate. https://www.bankrate.com/banking/cost-of-vacation/

Where to Exchange Currency Without Paying Huge Fees - Forbes Advisor. (n.d.). Www.forbes.com. https://www.forbes.com/advisor/money-transfer/money-transfer-where-to-exchange-currency/

explore, L. (2023, November 18). *A Comprehensive Guide to Planning and Budgeting for Long-Term Travel.* Medium.

Patrick Karban

https://lifeexplore.medium.com/a-comprehensive-guide-to-planning-and-budgeting-for-long-term-travel-c2b033c0d125

CBI. (2020, June 8). *How to manage risks in tourism? | CBI - Centre for the Promotion of Imports from developing countries.* Www.cbi.eu. https://www.cbi.eu/market-information/tourism/how-manage-risks-tourism

Help And Training Community. (n.d.). Salesforce. Retrieved August 1, 2024, from https://help.salesforce.com/s/articleView?id=release-notes.rn_fieldservice_250_travel_buffer.htm&language=en_US&release=250&type=5

Jovanović, P., Kecman, P., Bojović, N., & Mandić, D. (2017, January 1). *Optimal allocation of buffer times to increase train schedule robustness.* European Journal of Operational Research. https://doi.org/10.1016/j.ejor.2016.05.013

Cat. (2024, July 11). *How to Stay Healthy While Traveling - Wellness on the Go.* Coffee & Mascara. https://coffeeandmascara.org/how-to-stay-healthy-while-traveling-wellness-on-the-go/

Li, X., Zhou, J., & Zhao, X. (2016, September). *Travel itinerary problem.* Transportation Research Part B: Methodological. https://doi.org/10.1016/j.trb.2016.05.013

Practice, C. S., MD, Family Medicine, Nuvance Health Medical. (2024, July 30). *Nuvance Health - Tips to Stay Healthy During Your Vacation.* Good Morning Wilton. https://goodmorningwilton.com/vacation-health-tips-nuvance-health-sponsored-content-july-30-2024/

Reyes, J. (2023, March 13). *What is Supply Chain Disruption?* SafetyCulture. https://safetyculture.com/topics/supply-chain-disruption/

TripIt: Travel Planner. (2023, July 31). App Store. https://apps.apple.com/us/app/tripit-travel-planner/id311035142

The Best Travel Apps for 2022. (n.d.). PCMAG. https://www.pcmag.com/picks/best-travel-apps

Woods, C. (2023, June 21). *5 Essential Tips for Efficient Route Planning.* Locate2u. https://www.locate2u.com/route-planning/5-essential-tips-for-efficient-route-planning/

How to Get Over Jet Lag: 8 Tips and Suggestions. (2020, April 27). Healthline. https://www.healthline.com/health/healthy-sleep/how-to-get-over-jet-lag

LetsGetChecked. (2023, July 18). *How to Maintain Healthy Habits While Traveling.* LetsGetChecked; LetsGetChecked. https://www.letsgetchecked.com/articles/how-to-maintain-healthy-habits-while-traveling/

Medical Information for U.S. visitors to the United Kingdom. (n.d.). U.S. Embassy & Consulates in the United Kingdom. https://uk.usembassy.gov/u-s-citizen-services/medical-information/

Suni, E. (2021, February 5). *Jet lag: Symptoms: Causes, and How to Cope | Sleep Foundation.* Sleep Foundation. https://www.sleepfoundation.org/travel-and-sleep/jet-lag

Tips for Healthy, Happy Travels. (n.d.). Rick Steves. https://www.ricksteves.com/travel-tips/health/staying-healthy

Travel Insurance, Travel Health Insurance & Medical Evacuation Insurance | CDC Yellow Book 2024. (n.d.).

189

Wwwnc.cdc.gov. https://wwwnc.cdc.gov/travel/yellowbook/2024/health-care-abroad/insurance

Travel Medical Insurance Emergency Healthcare Coverage. (n.d.). MarketWatch - Guides. Retrieved August 1, 2024, from https://www.marketwatch.com/guides/insurance-services/travel-medical-insurance/

Your Health Abroad. (n.d.). Travel.state.gov. https://travel.state.gov/content/travel/en/international-travel/before-you-go/your-health-abroad.html

foreverroamingtheworld. (2017). *10 easy ways to overcome communication & language problems traveling - Forever roaming the world*. Www.foreverroamingtheworld.com. https://www.foreverroamingtheworld.com/language-problems-while-traveling/

thecurioussparrow. (2022, July 31). *How To Deal With Language Barriers While Traveling Abroad*. The Curious Sparrow. https://curioussparrowtravel.com/2022/07/31/how-to-deal-with-language-barriers-while-travelling-abroad/

Navigating Travel Advisories With Confidence: Your Guide to a Safe and Enjoyable Trip. https://frayedpassport.com/navigating-travel-advisories-with-confidence-your-guide-to-a-safe-and-enjoyable-trip/

Stress Reduction Strategies for Lawyers During High-Pressure Cases. https://calmegg.com/meditation-for-lawyers-and-legal-professionals/

Great Glen Way Baggage Transfer, East Highland Way, Loch Ness 360. https://www.piggybackbaggagetransfers.com/

How To Design A Landscape With Trees | urdesignmag. https://www.urdesignmag.com/how-to-design-a-landscape-with-trees/

Stay Up-To-Date With Weather News: http//weathernews.auone.jp/au/pollen/push.htmlarea14?rf=android app - Love Lola Blog. https://lovelolablog.com/2023/04/29/stay-up-to-date-with-weather-news-http-3a-weathernews-auone-jp-au-pollen-push-html-3farea-3d14-rf-androidapp/

How to Maintain Healthy Habits While Traveling. https://www.letsgetchecked.com/articles/how-to-maintain-healthy-habits-while-traveling/

191

9 783690 620000